THE ARAB SPRING & THE GULF STATES
TIME TO EMBRACE CHANGE

THE ARAB SPRING & THE GULF STATES

TIME TO EMBRACE CHANGE

Mohamed A. J. Althani

P

PROFILE BOOKS

First published in Great Britain in 2012 by
PROFILE BOOKS LTD
3A Exmouth House
Pine Street
London EC1R 0JH

www.profilebooks.com

1 3 5 7 9 10 8 6 4 2

A CIP catalogue record for this book is available from the British Library.

ISBN 978 1 78125 073 0
eISBN 978 1 84765 914 9

Maps by ML Design
Typeset in Bembo by MacGuru Ltd
info@macguru.org.uk

Printed and bound in Britain by Clays, Bungay, Suffolk

To Hamad bin Khalifa al-Thani, The Emir of the State of Qatar:
A man of courage, and a leader into prosperity and growth

CONTENTS

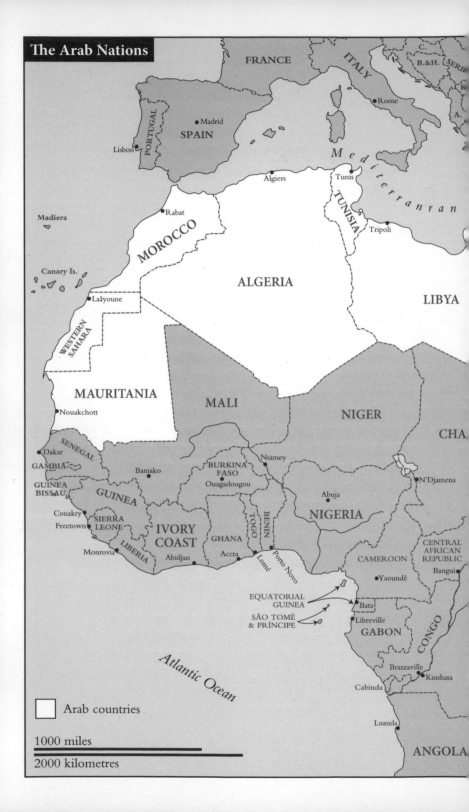

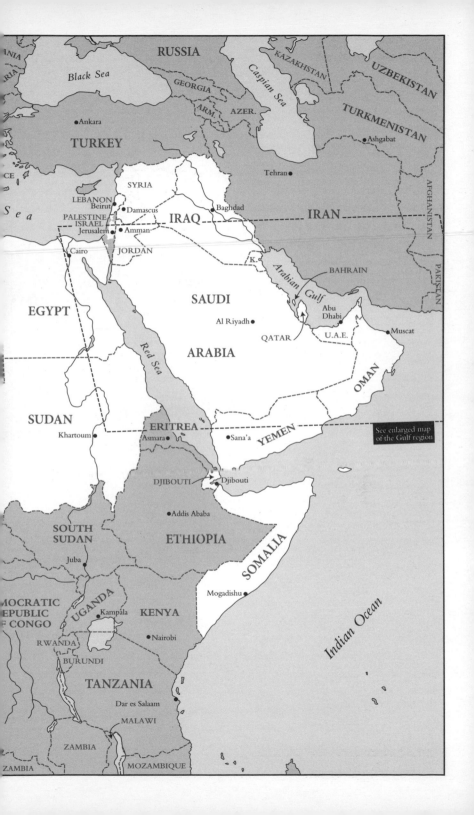

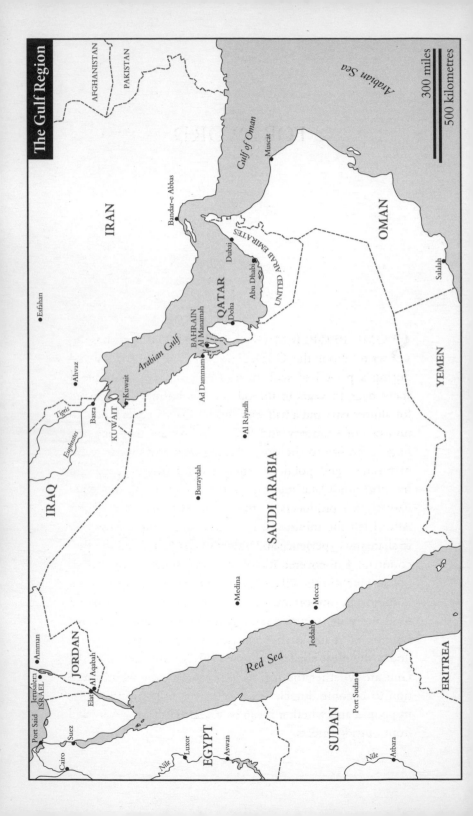

FOREWORD

SOME PEOPLE MIGHT WONDER why I chose to write about the Gulf economies and the Arab world during a period of such turmoil. The answer is simple. I spent over 17 years in the oil and gas business and served for almost two and a half years in the Qatari government as minister of economy and trade. This perspective gave me huge exposure to the domestic, regional and global world of business and politics. I am proud of playing a part in transforming Qatar into one of the biggest LNG (liquefied natural gas) producers in the world within a short time. After I left the ministry I decided to think about how best to share my experience and how it could be applied to other countries. I discovered that there was a shortage of analysis not so much in the oil and gas sectors as in the rather more domestically important areas of demography, security, and food and water security, and that the political and economic systems of many Arab countries were not well covered. Today, the most challenging questions for any citizen in the Gulf are whether the region is heading in the right direction to become durable and sustainable, fully supported by its people, and whether it can be defended domestically and from outside threats.

This book started during a fellowship I took at the Oxford Centre for Islamic Studies after I was asked to leave the ministry during 2006. I will never forget the day I was assigned to go to Sudan to prepare for an Arab League meeting of heads of state. After a routine cabinet meeting in Doha on Wednesday 23 March 2006, as I rushed to join my waiting delegation and board the plane, I was called in and advised that I would be replaced by another minister the following week. My first question was: did I do anything wrong? The answer was no, you have done a good job, but it is time for a change. Then I asked if I should go to Sudan or just call everything off and go home. Many things were going through my mind, but I realised that I must finish this last task and then think about other things (how to break this to my family and friends, and the ambitions I had for my institution). That trip was my hardest experience, because I had to conceal the situation from my family and the delegation to keep things under control until I got back.

I had joined a ministry where the bare minimum was being delivered, with 300 civil servants used to bureaucracy at its peak. When I left everything was electronic; commercial registrations that had previously taken two months to complete were issued in an hour. I had established from scratch a greenfield financial centre, a well-regulated stock exchange and a fully functional institution with highly motivated staff. Our revenues were double our annual expenditure.

Since childhood, I have learned not to look back and just carry on. What helped me through was the love of my wife and children who stayed close. Out of the 300 staff, only three have remained close friends; the rest just disappeared.

I had been working on a study concerning the political economy of the Gulf states at Oxford, but the financial crisis of 2008 hit just as my book was about to be reviewed for publication, rendering my forecasts and numbers irrelevant. I continued to update the study, but now it included coverage of the

Arab spring phenomenon and the associated alarm bells of youth unemployment, lack of participation, marginalisation of institutional effectiveness and ultimate powers over state resources. While at present the study is in English, I hope it will soon be translated into Arabic.

On 13 January 2011, I participated in a round table conference organised by the *Financial Times* on the future of the Gulf states. The agenda covered the need to create jobs, the risks of unemployment and the need for economic diversification. Unbelievably, that very month the Arab world would start to wake up from nearly 60 years of dormancy. Arabs have demanded freedom, an end to tyranny and improvements in their standard of living. One of the main sources for this book was interviews with people from the inner circle of the Arab ruling elites. I also spoke to people in other walks of life who agreed to give their views anonymously.

The main concern I have, and it is one I hope I have expressed in this book, is that we need to learn from the mistakes of others. We need the courage and honesty to implement real reform, admit our mistakes, come to terms with the reality of being behind, and put in place the right plan and strategy to achieve prosperity, social justice and equality within the rule of law.

For the Arab spring to succeed, elected parties and groups will have to navigate carefully through religious, ethnic and tribal divisions. This will require education and the creation of a functional civil society. In those countries that have not experienced any democratic movement, opposition leaders will need to make the first move towards managed political change. This change should ensure transition to a democracy in which everyone is equal, with respect for the rule of law and property rights. Meanwhile, institutions must be created to safeguard the next generation's interests.

My memories of change in the Gulf

I would like now to recount my memories of growing up in Qatar. I hope this will give readers some idea of how far the country has come.

I was born in Qatar during the early 1960s, becoming aware of my surroundings from about 1966. I did not grow up in the capital, Doha, but in what was then the small village of Al-Khor, now Qatar's second city. I feel fortunate that I had the opportunity to grow up where I did. In that small village we had only one school. As we grew it had to be enlarged to accommodate the increasing number of local students. Only elementary classes were taught in Al-Khor. All the secondary schools were in Doha, and to get there students were taken in trucks with neither seats nor air conditioning, sitting on the floor in the back covered with a tarpaulin to protect them from the sun. The journey would take about an hour because the lack of roads meant that much of it involved off-road driving. Students from Al-Khor slept in a dormitory in Doha for six days a week, going home on Thursday night and returning to the capital on Friday evenings. Formal education was a novelty for most of Qatari society, which meant that some students, having got the chance to start school only later in life, were considerably older than the rest of us.

Even in Al-Khor, getting to school was not easy for many students, especially those who lived in more remote areas. For some of those who lived in the desert the daily drive would take an hour because there were no paved roads. These students had to get up as early as 4am in order to be in class by 6.30am. My family was fortunate enough to have a car to drive us to school, though sometimes we would walk. When I was growing up there were not many cars on the street, making Al-Khor a quiet place. Hardly anyone else in the village was driven to school; most people walked or took the one old bus, which all too often would break down.

In those days education was limited to Arabic, Islamic studies and some science and mathematics. The teachers were mainly Palestinian refugees, most of whom had fled their homes following the 1967 war with Israel; but there were some who had fled the 1948–9 conflict. There was a small minority of Jordanian and Egyptian teachers.

There were no English classes during the first six years of my education. We started English in secondary school but the curriculum was limited. In one year the English course consisted of a simple short story, which we had to be able to read, and no grammar instruction at all. My first English teacher, an Egyptian, did not actually speak English; all he knew about the language was a few rules of grammar. We had an advantage as my elder brother was interested in reading English, so he provided us with magazines and simple books. He was largely self-taught, having been attracted by the variety of books available in English. Despite my brother's help, and that of an Indian engineer who worked on a construction site near our home and taught us a few basic words, I did not read English books often and therefore learned little of the language until later in life.

School started early in the morning and finished at 11.30am Our classes were crowded, with as many as 40 students, and facilities were minimal: a blackboard to study from and paper and booklets to write on. Pencils were so valuable that if you lost one you would be in trouble with your parents. We mostly learned by memory and there was very little to develop the mind. As long as you remembered exactly what was in the book, a pass grade would be granted. It was a case of memorising what they wanted you to learn. We also had three or four hours a week of what was called physical education. Mainly they gave us a ball and we would play in the sand or on the stony playground.

My feeling is that after oil revenues started flowing in the 1960s, the government was generous with students, but it simply did not have enough teachers to provide a proper education. The state used to give students pocket money and even materials with which they could have their own *dishdashas* and shoes made. But there was no after-class tutoring, so we had to be self-motivated to learn and do our homework.

Many parents were keen for their children to go to school because they had never had that opportunity. My father's biggest priority in life was for us to get an education. He felt that whatever the Ministry of Education – or the Department of Knowledge, as it used to be called in Arabic – chose as the curriculum was the best thing for us to study. I was lucky as my father had learned to read and write through his Koranic studies, but my mother had no formal education. And yet all of us, five boys and two girls, obtained university degrees; my youngest sister got a degree in medicine and became a consultant pathologist.

I spent many evenings sitting with my father and I learned a lot from him. I remember him saying that he used to walk along the shores of Qatar, especially in the north, looking for anything the sea washed up, especially driftwood. Sometimes a dhow would sink and they would find washed-up rice or vegetables. Once – it must have been around the late 1940s – he was walking near Ras Laffan, near where the Industrial City is today, and he found a half-rotten fruit he didn't recognise. He was hungry and since the fruit didn't smell too bad, he washed it with seawater, cut it up with a knife and ate it. Many years later he learned that this was the first time he tasted an apple. The sea was a big help to us as my father was a trader involved in the pearl industry. He would sail out to sea in a small boat to look for the captain of a pearling vessel. He would then purchase the pearls at his own risk, hoping to find buyers once he was back on land.

When we were attending school in Al-Khor, we would head home after class and the whole family would be waiting for us to have lunch together. Meals were quick and simple. Rice was a staple, as was meat from the animals that we raised and slaughtered at home; we never bought goats or meat from outside. We also had some fish, but poultry was not available until the 1970s.

We did not have freezers because electricity supplies were insufficient. The same applied to air conditioners, so until 1976 we slept outside during the summer, going to bed as early as possible so we could benefit from as many hours of the cooler night air as possible.

In the early 20th century the typical diet in Qatar was even more basic. Preserved dates were the main staple, most of them imported from other countries in the region such as Iraq and Saudi Arabia. There were only a few date plantations in Qatar. People relied on milk from cattle, goats or, if they were fortunate, camels that they raised. Rice was imported from India, smuggled sugar was a highly prized commodity and coffee was a luxury.

The takeover by Sheikh Khalifa bin Hamad al-Thani in 1971 brought positive changes, and living conditions in Qatar began to improve significantly in 1973–4. We saw a difference after the first oil shock in 1973 when world energy prices rose, resulting in a marked increase in national income. Even greater progress followed the oil boom of 1976, especially after the Iranian revolution.

Nonetheless, we did not have telephones in my village until 1978, so it was a problem for us when my brother went to study in the UK in 1976. My father had to drive to the cable and wireless office in Doha, where he would enter a cubicle to call my brother in London, hoping to catch him at home with his host family. We had a black-and-white television by then, although there was controversy in some homes over whether this medium of news and entertainment was permissible. My first experience of colour TV was about 1978. For several years the only programming we could watch was that aired on the Saudi Aramco channel. There was nothing in Arabic; everything was in English, although some programmes had subtitles. Even though the channel transmitted only between 5pm and 8pm, we found it entertaining. At some point in the 1970s we were able to tune in to Kuwaiti broadcasts, but our antennas had to be positioned just right, and frequently there was no reception.

In several respects, 1979 was a landmark year for me. I finished my secondary schooling in the summer and embarked on a foreign education. My first proper English studies started at the language centre at the University of California at Los Angeles (UCLA) in early October. Despite my personal development, I had mixed feelings about the world around me at that time. The Islamic Revolution in Iran and the rise to power of Ayatollah Ruhollah Khomeini was an eye-opener. I started to worry about the geopolitical problems surrounding the Gulf region, realising the precariousness of Qatar's position.

Growing up in the 1960s and 1970s, my concerns had been far simpler, and my father recalled a time of even more basic fears. He had lived through a period of virtual famine between the First World War and the Second World War, and he worried about things that my brothers and I considered irrelevant. Behind our home in Al-Khor we had about 300 camels, 60 head of cattle, and 400 sheep and goats that he had raised and would not let go, even in the 1980s. All this livestock was a costly burden for us; in the past they had largely been left to survive on their own in the desert, but now we had to keep them in enclosures, which took time and money.

My father had a different perspective. Born in 1913, he was of a generation that had experienced hard times and considered livestock a crucial means of guaranteeing one's survival. It was difficult to convince him to get rid of his animals, which he considered his life savings. He raised us on the principle that money was not as important as having access to food and water. He liked having a large farm that produced natural and organic foods. He also kept bees, and generally his goal was to ensure that we had enough stocks of honey, wheat and dates to last us for two years, even though he gave away large amounts of dates to other families.

At that time our farm produced about 3,000 kilograms of dates a year, and he used to follow their development daily. In the morning he would wake up early and go to a makeshift office that he shared with friends before finishing a few chores. He would rest in the early afternoon then go to the farm to check on his crops, particularly the date crop, which needed to be well protected. Date palms yield fruit only once a year, so he took special care of them. The date harvest is between June and September, a crucial period for him.

I remember travelling all over Qatar with my father on hunting trips, for which we hired a guide. Hunting was a big part of our lives and my father loved it. He had hunted deer in Iran, and birds with falcons in Iraq. He went as far as Syria in the 1970s, but his more regular trips were to Saudi Arabia. These took place during the winter and typically lasted for three months, so he was happy when we were old enough to write him letters while he was away. Every two or three weeks he would send a driver from Saudi Arabia to bring us the birds and other animals that he had bagged, along with a letter. I would send the driver back with whatever he required and a reply to his letter. The only other way to communicate with him would involve someone driving 2,000 kilometres to the northern part of Saudi Arabia. The cars were mainly Land Rovers, but the terrain and inadequate roads meant they couldn't travel faster than 70 kilometres per hour, so it took a long time to travel to Iraq or Saudi Arabia.

When we drove through our own Qatari desert it was rare to see a car, as most people could not afford one. The same applied to hunting trips, which were limited to sheikhs and a few others with enough money. There were few police. Most of the police officers in Qatar came from Yemen and they were peaceful and reliable. The country was safe and people had little to fear, as there was virtually no crime.

In the 1960s it was common to see people riding donkeys and camels. Animals were used to transport water, which was scarce because it was mostly taken from wells. There were no pumps, so people used to carry water by hand to tanks on the roofs of their houses, from where it entered the plumbing system.

It was interesting to observe the relationship between my father and mother. They grew up during a period of great hardship and lived long enough to see the growth of the country and the money that started to flow in. Yet they never wasted food or money; everything was carefully calculated and we used to say that you could set a clock by the older people's routine. This would be the same every day: not just waking up and going to sleep at the same time, but organising every detail of life to make each day more efficient and more fruitful. They would not understand the lives we live today.

It's sad to see the younger generation forgetting these values and living the easy life, often without appreciating it. When my generation was growing up our parents were keen to see us get an education because they did not have that opportunity. Money was far less important for them than our schooling; they wanted us to do something good for ourselves and for our country. I think that was a good approach to life.

Our generation has done well. Many Qataris have gone to the US or Europe to study and have returned as qualified economists, lawyers, engineers and so on with much to contribute. Members of our generation have educated themselves – an impressive achievement when one considers that most of their parents could not read or write. However, once they became educated and started to have children, their mentality changed and the next generation has different priorities. Many parents now think that the best thing for their children is to make as much money as possible and to secure their lives in financial terms. The top priorities are to own a home and have an extensive investment portfolio.

This attitude has made the younger generation complacent. When children look at their parents and see that they lack nothing, there is a tendency to overlook the value of real learning and hard work. We have young men whose main goal is just to secure whatever job they can, especially in the public sector, and do as little work as possible while enjoying the good life. Owning flashy cars and travelling with their friends have become the priorities for these people, and that is one change that is not positive.

The other change is that while people are still keen on education, there has been an increase in the popularity of Western-style learning. Nowadays parents send their children to English- or French-language schools from the start, which means they are torn between their own language and culture and that of the people who design and deliver their education. This is worrying for many parents as they realise that their teenage children are not well adjusted to their own culture, language or heritage. They feel embarrassed because their children do not speak good Arabic. The same is true for parents who raise their children outside their own country. Some people have recognised the problem and there has been a reversal in the trend towards sending children to foreign-language schools, but it remains a challenge. This has become more problematic since 9/11, particularly as some states have reformed education by following the American model.

It is difficult for young people to build their identity and their attachment to the state. What are their main concerns for the future? For people in the 1960s and 1970s, the Palestinian issue was everything. Now the priorities and mentalities of young people are different, and I am not at all sure that this is a good thing. I believe strongly that you need to maintain some fundamental principles and therefore to make some issues a permanent priority. After that you can concentrate on new ideas.

Is it good for us, this period of rapid growth with all the changes that have taken place within Gulf societies? I think so. If we set our people on the right track, they can benefit from what has become available. As I have mentioned, there was no home telephone service in my village until 1978, but now we live in an age of instant communications with the internet, satellite TV and mobile phones. We should not fear this, but rather embrace it and take as much advantage of it as possible. This is a challenge that both the state and individuals must take up – and this must be in tandem with an effort to ensure that people retain their culture and heritage and build upon them.

The states and peoples of the Gulf can more easily accomplish these and related goals if they become more open to – and reliant on – each other. In the 1960s and 1970s in Qatar we had no Indian or Filipino workers, only workers from Bahrain, Iran, Oman, Yemen and what is now the United Arab Emirates (UAE). Many senior people from Abu Dhabi studied in Qatar before Sheikh Zayed bin Sultan al-Nahyan took over and launched the development programme that continues today.

I remember when it was easy to go to Saudi Arabia, Kuwait, Bahrain or the UAE. My first plane trip was a flight to Bahrain operated by a British company. I also remember going to Bahrain aboard a dhow that sailed from the northern tip of Qatar. Other forms of transport included trucks going to Saudi Arabia. It was not a difficult process: you could cross any border and no one would stop you. In those days Qatar had enough agricultural production to allow exports to Saudi Arabia; this really stands out in my mind because today Qatar imports all its food. Our population was much smaller and winter rainfall was more reliable, but we had only basic equipment like pumps to water our crops, not the modern irrigation technology available today. More importantly, our own people – and our guests – had more industrious habits and faced fewer restrictions. There were Palestinian families who took over farms and went straight to work, planting whatever they could and learning as they went.

I worry that the current generation is too complacent to do anything so productive. I also fear that too much foreign education has crept into our culture and our lives. It is important to learn English and French, but we should make sure that our children's education is based on their own language and culture. We should also make sure that foreigners understand that if and when we begin to reduce the teaching of their languages in our schools, it is not through disdain for their culture but through concern for our own. I am also deeply concerned about such matters as succession, and both economic and political stability. How do we make sure that there isn't another invasion of Kuwait or another meltdown in Dubai? If we openly share ideas among the leaders and peoples of the region, I think we can avoid such setbacks and start planning for a more stable future.

We have come a long way during my lifetime, not solely because of the energy reserves under our feet and the appetites and ingenuities of foreigners; much of the development we have achieved has been the result of thoughtful leadership and our own hard work. To build sensibly on this foundation, however, we must avoid the self-satisfaction and consumerism that can only contribute to further complacency. We need, too, to recognise that criticism of current or past leaders stems not from a deficit of pride in one's country and one's civilisation but, on the contrary, from a surfeit thereof. We need to combine sober analysis with free thinking, to openly discuss our current situation and our goals for the future, if we are to arrive at workable solutions to our own problems. I hope that in some small way this book will contribute to that process.

1970–2011: FOUR DECADES OF TRANSFORMATION IN THE GULF

OVER THE PAST 40 YEARS, the Gulf states have transformed themselves from sleepy, obscure sheikhdoms into modern states with global influence. The transformation has been swift, and the Gulf Co-operation Council (GCC) states have experienced some of the most rapid spurts of development and economic growth in recent global history. In this relatively short period, they have made huge progress in terms of public health, standards of living, education, the creation of institutions and state building.

Before the 1970s, standards of living in the Gulf states were poor. There is no shortage of indicators to prove this: in Saudi Arabia in 1970 the literacy rate was 15 per cent for men and 2 per cent for women;[1] and in 1960 in the UAE the infant mortality rate was 145 per 1,000.[2]

Politically, the Gulf states were fragile. The older countries in the region, such as Kuwait and Saudi Arabia, were slowly building state institutions and enforcing state control in all their territories. The younger ones, such as Bahrain, Qatar and the UAE, only achieved independence from British rule in 1971 and were just beginning the process of state building. In most Arabian states the lack of institutions meant that the ruler and his immediate circle controlled all deci-sion-making, even in unimportant matters.

Arabian society was largely untouched by modernisation before the 1970s, relying on traditional forms of social organisa-tion. Tribal structures were important. Since the crash of the pearl market in the 1930s, the economies of the region had been sluggish. Many inhabitants had a semi-subsistence lifestyle, with income from farms and livestock and any work they could find.

The Gulf oil industry started in the 1940s, but it was not until the 1970s that it began to generate revenues that could be distrib-uted among the states' inhabitants. This income allowed the Gulf states to take the first steps towards the transformation of their economies. In 1972 the Arab oil embargo meant that the price of oil quadrupled to almost $12 a barrel. As a result, oil revenues in Saudi Arabia rose from $4.3bn in 1973 to $101.8bn in 1980.[3] Similar increases occurred in the other Gulf states.

With the rise in oil revenues, government spending increased rapidly. There was investment in infrastructure projects such as roads, hospitals and schools, which encouraged many of the region's inhabitants to become more loyal to their state. Mer-chants set up companies to take advantage of government spend-ing on infrastructure. These companies, many of which are still in business today, formed the basis of the modern private sector in the region. The huge increase in demand for food, vehicles, consumer goods and other products meant that many of these merchant families and their royal patrons became very wealthy in a short period of time.

The second Gulf oil boom

Since 2000, the Gulf states have experienced a second oil boom. At its peak, prices hit $140 a barrel. This boom had similar effects to that of the 1970s. GDP per head rose further and in some cases became among the highest in the world. Massive government spending pushed economies into double-digit growth.

The region attracted publicity as some of its more ambitious leaders sought to develop their countries into world centres. Building projects such as the Burj Khalifa tower and Palm islands in Dubai captured the world's imagination and hastened the development of the Gulf tourism industry. Other countries in the region devised aggressive investment plans and acquired assets throughout the world.

By the middle of the 2000s, optimism throughout the Gulf was high. Government investment drove growth and GCC citizens, as well as many foreign residents, experienced unprecedented affluence. Banks embarked on aggressive campaigns to expand their loan portfolios and businesses and individuals became increasingly comfortable with highly leveraged positions.

These developments were accompanied by keenly optimistic predictions about the region's future. These were often built on the premise that the Gulf's strategic position at the crossroads between Asia, Europe and Africa could make it a global hub for services and trade. In July 2008, Nasser al Saidi, chief economist of the Dubai International Finance Centre, predicted that the GCC would become the world's fifth biggest economy by 2020.[4]

Even when the global economic crisis intensified after the collapse of Lehman Brothers in September 2008, many felt that the GCC would remain immune. However, the effects of the recession were quickly felt across the region. Oil prices fell from highs of $147 a barrel to less than $38 in January 2009, and the region's exposure to Western stock markets and other assets left both individuals and institutions nursing serious losses. As some countries entered recession, loan portfolios started to perform poorly and some banks needed government support to survive.

Businesses that had enjoyed years of strong growth suddenly had to learn to operate in a downturn, and governments had to adapt to managing recession. Dubai, which had developed the most high-profile image in the region, mainly as a result of huge real estate projects, soon encountered significant problems. Real estate prices fell rapidly and the economy started to contract. The emirate still looks fragile, with its flagship company, Dubai World, seeking to restructure billions of dollars of debt.

The recession demonstrated that although much had been accomplished in the previous ten years, the Gulf states remain vulnerable to shocks in the global economy, making the need to diversify away from a reliance on oil income more pressing than ever.

The diversification struggle

Economic diversification away from oil revenues has been a mantra repeated by Gulf policymakers for several decades. In many respects the region has made real progress. Between 2002 and 2008, the GCC's non-oil sector is believed to have grown at an annual rate of about 7.5 per cent.[5]

Increasingly, the Gulf's private sector is becoming more powerful and confident. GCC companies now have footholds across the Middle East and are gaining access to Western and emerging markets. Firms are strengthening their corporate structure and some have listed on stock markets. Management standards have improved and a number of GCC citizens are obtaining MBAs as well as experience in multinational companies. Many of these firms are able to operate in Middle Eastern markets where cultural and political restrictions make things difficult for Western companies. As the private sector has grown, there has also been growth in trade within the GCC. Between 2000 and 2005, inter-Arab trade tripled, although around half of this consisted of oil.

However, despite growth in the private sector, government investment still plays a huge role in the economy. Over the next five years it is estimated that the total value of public and private investment in the GCC will be $1.9 trillion, and 65 per cent of this will be spent on infrastructure.[6] These large projects are aimed at diversifying the economy away from oil, and billions are being invested in tourism, airlines, industry and transport infrastructure.

There are many impediments to growth in the private sector. Although GCC states have taken steps towards cutting red tape and bureaucracy, their efforts have sometimes been in vain. Excessive bureaucracy is believed to be the reason foreign direct investment in Kuwait is lower than it is in Yemen.

Companies complain that it is hard to do business because of governmental failure to streamline procedures for obtaining work visas and import licences and the lack of action taken to ease the movement of goods across borders.[7] According to the World Bank, the highest-ranking Middle Eastern country in its most recent 'Ease of Doing Business Survey' was Saudi Arabia, with a global ranking of 13.[8] This is lower than Asian countries such as Singapore, China and Thailand, all of which have experienced strong economic growth over the past decade.

Despite some improvements, governments in the region have been unable to shape their policies to suit the needs of the private sector. Decision making processes have been clouded by political and security factors that restrict new measures on issues such as open borders. For example, friction between Saudi Arabia and Qatar has at times prevented a lifting of restrictions that would make it easier for commercial businesses to cross their shared border.[9]

Another effect of the lack of democratic structures and procedure in the region has been a lack of transparency in decision-making. Government bodies and those who run them are not always accountable; in some cases in the GCC, ministers have been in their ministries for years. In many states, a handful of individuals from the ruling elite dominate certain sectors and protect monopolies at the expense of other businesspeople who want to enter markets and offer new products and services that would compete with the established order.

A rentier class

Since the discovery of oil, a 'rentier class' has developed which generates an income through the collection of 'rents'. These include providing agencies for foreign companies that wish to operate in GCC states, sponsoring foreign workers' permits in return for fees, and real estate ownership and speculation. Other forms of rent gathering include taking commissions from foreign companies seeking contracts with the government. The GCC region also has a large number of financiers who invest in projects but do not take an active role in their development.

The rentier class limits economic development as it undermines productivity and provides minimal incentives for risk-taking. Its existence has prevented the development of a large entrepreneur class with the ambition to accomplish more than the collection of rents. There are many examples of GCC citizens who are successful entrepreneurs, but these are few considering the resources and education available to them.

Another hurdle for the private sector has been the workforce nationalisation policies in all GCC countries, brought in to reduce dependence on expatriate workers. These policies are a necessity and in some cases have been implemented successfully. However, the system of imposing hiring quotas on private-sector companies has its flaws. It has caused a malaise among some citizens, who feel they are entitled to jobs in the private sector. It has been difficult for these nationals to be sacked, and therefore many have had little incentive to perform to the best of their ability.

For decades there have been anecdotal stories about nationals arriving at work late and having much of their work done by expatriates, who are cheaper and more efficient to employ. This phenomenon has been bad for the private sector. It has also had a negative effect on the development of GCC nationals, who have not been forced to give of their best because they have been subject to lower benchmarks than those set for expatriate workers.

Another aspect of this problem is the patronage networks within the public and private sectors, which mean that people are hired not necessarily on the basis of competence or skills but because of their connections. This creates a malaise among the local workforce, who feel that they are either guaranteed a job because of their standing in society or disenfranchised because of their lower standing and therefore have no incentive to work hard or gain new skills.

Planning for a post-oil future

One of the realities in the Gulf is that oil is a finite resource that will eventually be depleted. Furthermore, as oil becomes more expensive there is a greater economic incentive to develop alternative energy sources that would reduce its value. As a result, governments in the region have established sovereign wealth funds (SWFs) designed to protect them against fluctuations in oil and gas prices and safeguard the future of their economies when hydrocarbon reserves run out. Over the years, these SWFs have been allotted a percentage of oil revenues and have grown to a significant size. Accordingly, their activities have generated considerable attention around the world.

SWFs operate in various ways. Some have low profiles and low-risk strategies that avoid majority stakes in companies and focus on assets perceived to be secure, such as US Treasury bonds. Abu Dhabi, Saudi Arabia and Kuwait have traditionally preferred this strategy. Others have sought controlling stakes in high-profile Western companies and have adopted a type of private-equity strategy involving high degrees of leverage. Dubai and Qatar have generally followed this strategy.

GCC SWFs have invested significant amounts in Western economies and their role is treated with a mixture of suspicion and appreciation. Before the recession, their presence was thought to be threatening: many Western governments were concerned that they might use investments in strategic assets for political gain. Following the recession, Western policymakers were keen to encourage their investment in the badly damaged banking sector.

Generally, GCC governments have seen Western assets as stable, reliable investments. The accusation that they have a hidden political agenda is unfounded and, with the exception of the 1970s oil embargo, which is now widely considered to have been a mistake, all GCC states have proven to be reliable energy exporters to Western countries. Their reliability in this regard should be considered a sign of their SWFs' intentions.

However, these institutions are characterised by a damaging lack of transparency. The value, performance and specific details of SWF investments are not made public. Assessments of their size vary wildly and in the case of the Abu Dhabi Investment Authority estimates range from $650bn to $875bn.[10]

Outside the GCC, the management of SWFs is subject to public scrutiny. For example, the Government Pension Fund in Norway is one of the largest equity owners in Europe, with a total value of $455bn as at the end of 2008. Governed by an ethics committee, which ensures its investments remain within established guidelines, the fund is the subject of regular debate in Norway and is wholly transparent.

The lack of transparency in Gulf SWFs is a serious problem for GCC countries, as the primary function of these funds is to safeguard each state's future. That they are not run in a manner that allows public scrutiny clearly threatens this aim. In the worst case, this lack of transparency could lead to money being siphoned off. Ideally, SWFs should be transparently managed and non-political. Moreover, although the recession has lessened objections to Gulf investment in the West, concerns over investor intentions could be eased if these SWFs had more effective public relations policies – a development that would go hand in hand with improved transparency.

Absence of transparency has played a major role in moulding

the way Gulf economies are managed, and all the GCC countries have suffered as a result. Most of them are relatively young, and there has been little opportunity to develop the checks and balances seen in more mature societies. Breakneck development in recent years has catapulted the Gulf states into the modern era, but in terms of governance, practice has developed little and many decisions are made informally, often in a traditional fashion in which only the necessary stakeholders are consulted. As a result, there is a lack of clarity as to whether SWFs and other investment bodies are acting in the interests of the state or of individuals within the state. Several recent test cases have revealed that officials have invested their own money and that of the state in the same assets.

A tale of two Arab worlds

The rest of the Arab world has experienced a different type of governance. With the exception of Morocco and Jordan, most of the non-Gulf Arab states have been governed by republican systems with a president as head of state. There are several reasons why these states developed differently from the Gulf Arab countries.

Many of the republican systems are the consequence of the rise of nationalist post-colonial politics. After the end of colonial rule by European powers in the 1940s and 1950s, Arab nationalism became an important ideology and leaders such as Egypt's Gamal Abdel Nasser came to power. Arab nationalism was defined by the principles of Arab unity, cultural pride and resistance to Israel.

In the 1950s and 1960s these principles were popular and defined Arab politics. Nasser's power extended across the region and his message even penetrated the Gulf societies, where the conservative monarchies were on the defensive. There was tension between the Gulf monarchies and the nationalist republics, which some historians refer to as the 'Arab cold war'.

Following the defeat of the Arab forces in 1967, however, Arab nationalism began to find itself on the back foot. During the Cold War the US supported conservative monarchies against the republics, which it believed might back Soviet ambitions in the region. Later, the US also engaged with Islamism as it believed it too acted as a bulwark against communism.

After the 1970s, the republics began to decline. Although many of them claimed to be creating more progressive societies, they nonetheless became some of the worst regimes in the region. Baathist states such as Syria and Iraq have abused human rights on a massive scale. Many republics have become notorious for widespread corruption and poor governance. Countries such as Algeria, Lebanon, Yemen and Iraq have been devastated by conflicts. Others such as Egypt, Jordan and Tunisia have remained peaceful but with little achievement in terms of economic development or political improvements.

Aside from human rights and politics, all the non-Gulf Arab states face a serious economic crisis. More than one in four Arabs are out of work and it is estimated that more than 55 million new jobs will have to be created by 2020 to keep this number from growing. Often the talented and educated middle class leave to find jobs in the US and Europe, resulting in a brain drain estimated to cost Arab economies $1.6bn a year.[11]

In the face of this, there has been a lack of innovative ideas or policies. Many governments have not had the vision or the accountability to address unemployment and foster sustainable economic growth. A lack of democracy has resulted in public administrations that are not well audited and whose performance is measured by their ability to maintain stability rather than to introduce progressive policies.

The performance of governments has been poor and the years of damage will have to be undone. The region's inhabitants have had to deal with unemployment, corruption, nepotism and the absence of vision and competitive spirit. Upward mobility is difficult. Connections and influence are crucial to success. Jobs in the private and private sector are often accessed through patronage networks and this marginalises large sections of the population.

Population growth

One problem shared by all Arab states is population growth and a young demographic. Arab countries have some of the fastest growing populations in the world, as a result of high fertility rates and early marriage. Medical care has improved, which means life expectancy has increased by more than ten years since the 1980s.[12] So far there are few signs that Arab governments can curb population growth through family-planning programmes.

The population of the region is young; according to the United Nations, around half of the 350 million Arabs are aged under 25. This figure is expected to double by 2050 if current growth rates are sustained. Some figures are hard to credit: in Algeria, for example, it is estimated that 75 per cent of the population is under the age of 30.

Gulf population growth is around 2.5 per cent a year, and in North Africa it is around 2.2 per cent. Other Arab countries have a population growth rate of around 2.2 per cent a year. If these rates continue, it is estimated that the population of the Gulf countries could double within 30 years, and that of North Africa in around 50 years.[13]

Immigration strategies in several Gulf states are also affecting population growth. Countries such as the UAE have created freehold property that can be bought by non-GCC nationals, thus encouraging more people to live there.

Such population growth has many consequences. Arab governments face a huge challenge in terms of creating jobs for their growing populations, but they must also provide sufficient housing, infrastructure, schools and healthcare facilities. Increased

water and electricity supplies are also required so that Arab countries, many of which rely on imports, can ensure that they become
more self-sufficient in food.

2

THE ARAB SPRING

FOR THE ARAB WORLD, 2011 was a year of unimaginable change. In what was dubbed the 'Arab spring', four Arab leaders were overthrown in less than 12 months: Zine el-Abidine Ben Ali in Tunisia, Hosni Mubarak in Egypt, Muammar Qaddafi in Libya and Ali Abdullah Saleh in Yemen. The position of several others, including Bashar Assad in Syria, is threatened by uprisings.

These events were almost impossible to predict. But with hindsight it is clear that at some point the years of neglect, powerlessness, unemployment, high inflation, corruption and economic struggle would take their toll and Arabs would start to demand drastic change.

The status quo across the region looks under threat, and potentially all the Arab regimes will face a struggle to survive. There are several indications that citizens are no longer willing to accept the political pact that has defined their countries for decades. This shift in the region's political culture has taken less than a year. The Arab public has been emboldened and many people feel they must take their destiny into their own hands.

The Arab spring is almost certain to disappoint in the short term. The problems that Arab countries face cannot be solved by elections or a transition to a more democratic system. The reforms required for better governance and economic growth will take years to embed, and it will be long time before the sacrifices being made by Arab activists are rewarded.

The risks are potentially huge. The removal of regimes in power for decades could unleash the horrors of sectarianism, tribalism and chaos. This was clearly seen in Iraq when the removal of the Baathist regime resulted in a period of civil war. The Shia, for example, encouraged by Iran, sought vengeance on the Sunni community, which they blamed for persecution suffered under Saddam Hussein. The fall of the regime in 2003 also meant the collapse of the state, such that the government was unable to meet its people's basic needs. These problems persist almost ten years later.

Many states, such as Syria, Libya and Yemen, have similar divisions on sectarian and tribal lines. A peaceful and orderly transition will be challenging in these countries, and opposition movements should bear this in mind when or if they take power.

The Arab spring also provides a chance for the West as well as Iran, Turkey and other countries to intervene in Arab politics. This has already been seen in Libya, where the success of the NATO campaign served to vindicate the concept of 'humanitarian intervention'. This is a risk to the sovereignty and independence of Arab politics. Many would argue that foreign powers such as the US already have a huge influence on Arab governments. This may be the case, but historically Arab states have tended to become more sovereign since the end of the colonial period – progress that could potentially be undone by the Arab spring.

Why the Arab spring?

Why has the Arab spring taken place now? As noted in Chapter 1, Arab governments outside the Gulf have been in a state of slow decline for several years. Corruption, poor governance and a lack of accountability have left them unable to cope with the challenges of population growth, unemployment, environmental problems and poverty.

These problems are not new, however, and do not explain why in less than a year the region has experienced such rapid change. Analysts have offered several reasons, including economic hardship, the internet and media freedom. The debate over the causes of the Arab spring has even led some in the West to argue that the invasion of Iraq was justified and that the revolutions of 2011 were a delayed reaction to Saddam Hussein's fall in 2003.

Before the uprising in Syria in March 2011, many analysts predicted that President Assad and his regime would remain immune from political unrest because his foreign policy, which is perceived to be anti-Western and pro-Palestinian, had the approval of the majority of his people. This was quickly proved wrong.

In reality, there is not just one reason the Arab spring happened when it did; it was probably a combination of the factors mentioned above. Political unrest has different causes in different countries. Each revolution and opposition movement has its own local features, all of them unique. However, there are common features shared by all Arab countries, and it is these that have created the so-called 'domino effect'. Arabs have a shared culture despite their division by borders and states. They watch the same media and speak different dialects of the same language. It is ironic that several decades after Arab nationalism lost its popular appeal, Arab politics at state level is so sensitive to events taking place in other Arab countries.

The internet and the media have clearly helped to facilitate the Arab spring. Facebook, Twitter and other forums have allowed activists to organise and create alternative sources for news and information. Over the past five years, a rapid increase in the membership of sites such as Facebook has made it easier for information to spread efficiently. It has been relatively hard for Arab regimes to censor the internet and users have quickly learned how to access blocked sites.

The internet has its limitations. The countries that have experienced revolution have relatively low internet penetration rates. For example, in Egypt only around 25 per cent of citizens have access to the internet; in Tunisia it is slightly more at 35 per cent, but in Libya it is only 5 per cent.[1] And only 5 per cent of Egyptian and 4 per cent of Libyan internet users have Facebook accounts.[2] The internet has been used as a tool by middle-class activists; it has not been the chief factor behind the Arab spring.

Television channels, mainly Al Jazeera and Al Arabiya, have also played an important role. Al Jazeera has been generally enthusiastic about the revolutions of 2011. Al Arabiya has been far more cautious in its coverage of the Egyptian and Tunisian revolutions, but more aggressive in its reporting on Syria. Although these TV channels have undoubtedly played a role, they are driven as much by inter-Arab politics as free-minded journalism. Al Arabiya's owners are close to the Saudi government, which means its Arab political coverage tends to be conservative. Al Jazeera has more room for manoeuvre, but in some cases it reflects a certain regional foreign policy. The region is in need of more independent Arab media that can take an objective and consistent line during these polarised times.

An interesting media feature of the Arab spring has been WikiLeaks. Although it cannot take full credit for the Tunisian revolution, WikiLeaks played an important role by confirming to Tunisians what they already suspected. Some pundits dubbed the Tunisian revolution the 'first WikiLeaks revolution' in the belief that it was sparked by the release of US embassy cables in December 2010. The cables revealed harsh criticism of Tunisia's ruling elite by the US ambassador, and in some cases detailed cases of corruption that the embassy was aware of. One of the cables declared: 'Corruption in the inner circle is growing. Even average Tunisians are keenly aware of it, and the chorus of complaints is rising. Tunisians intensely dislike, even hate, first lady Leila Trabelsi and her family. In private, regime opponents mock her; even those close to the government express dismay at her reported behaviour.'

In terms of the standard of governance and its part in the events of 2011, there is no doubt that dissatisfaction with the status quo was a motivating factor. However, World Bank governance indicators for some countries in the region show little change over the past two decades. Tunisia, the country in which the Arab spring was born, had relatively high governance scores.

What has changed over the past two decades is population size. As noted in the previous chapter, the number of young people entering the job market has grown rapidly and this has put pressure on government bureaucracies. Traditionally, governments would absorb jobseekers in the public sector, while the private sector remained a relatively minor employer. But in all Arab countries the public sector is now struggling to absorb a sufficient number of jobseekers, and as the sector tends to rely on patronage networks, many people find themselves marginalised and excluded.

The Arab spring is largely the result of the Arab states' inability to deal with the growing numbers of young people. This has been exacerbated by external factors over which the state has little control. For example, in many Arab countries subsidies on basic goods and commodities have been lifted and rising food prices have made food and fuel expensive for those on low salaries.

As these states have liberalised their economies, the private sector has remained as dysfunctional as the bureaucracies that govern them. Across the Arab world there are examples of businessmen who are well-connected to the ruling elite and as a result control large sections of the economy in the manner of an oligarchy.

In Syria, Rami Makhlouf, the president's cousin, has stakes in mobile phone companies, banks, airlines, oil companies, insurance companies and a wide range of other businesses. The *Financial Times* estimates that he controls around 60 per cent of the Syrian economy and has the power to block the entry of foreign companies until they agree to partner with him.[3] Before the revolution in Tunisia, the family of the deposed president's wife, the Trabelsis, also played an oligarchic role, controlling a wide range of companies and often serving as partners for foreign companies.

There are many other such individuals in the Arab states and their dominance has stunted development of the private sector. Instead of fostering a more meritocratic culture, the private sector in many Arab states has mirrored the public sector. As a result, success is often dictated by sect, tribe and connections rather than talent and competitiveness.

Another important factor was the financial crisis of 2008. Outside the Gulf, many Arab economies were initially unscathed by the crisis as their banking sectors were not much exposed to banks in the West. Indeed, conservative governance of some of the region's banks, such as those in Lebanon, as well as Sharia-compliant institutions, meant that they gained from the crisis as their model was seen to be less risky than the West's.

The effects of the recession were seen in the decline in remittances from expatriate workers. Countries such as Morocco, Egypt, Tunisia, Lebanon and Syria have large numbers of workers in Europe and the Gulf and their economies rely on remittances. It is estimated that 2.7 million Egyptians work abroad – 70 per cent in other Arab countries and the remainder in Europe and the US – sending $7.8bn back to Egypt each year.[4] Other countries in the region are even more reliant on remittances: in 2009, Lebanon received $5.5bn from expatriates, a huge amount for a country of just 4 million people.[5]

Since the financial crisis, expatriate workers have either been laid off or have less money to send home. Remittances are informal and gauging them is difficult, but some analysts suggest that the number of non-Gulf Arab workers in the Gulf fell by as much as 30 per cent in 2009.[6] This fall in remittances has put further pressure on societies that were already dealing with unemployment and inflation.

Interestingly, it has often been argued that emigration serves as a pressure valve for Arab countries and thus helps regimes to survive. Thus emigration to the Gulf and Europe removed a middle class who would otherwise have been frustrated by the lack of opportunity at home and demanded political change. The reduction in job opportunities abroad as a result of the global recession is likely to have played a role in the Arab spring.

Age is another factor. The predominance of youth in Arab populations is in sharp contrast to their leaders. Hosni Mubarak was an octogenarian president of a country in which 31 per cent of the population were under the age of 15.[7] In Saudi Arabia and elsewhere, an elderly elite rules a youthful population. This factor can be overstated, however: Bashar Assad, the youngest Arab ruler, is in his mid-40s.

Western foreign policy must also take some responsibility for the sudden political change. The US and Europe have generally taken a 'stability first' approach in the region and have consistently supported autocratic regimes and leaders. This stems from a fear of Islamism, a preoccupation with oil and the important role that Israel plays in Western politics. As a result, there was little Western support for genuine reform to challenge the status quo. But the approach has proven unsustainable: meaningful reform was not encouraged as a path for change, leaving the only route a revolutionary and unmanaged one.

The shortcomings of this policy were evident during the Egyptian revolution, when US officials made crass remarks about their support for Mubarak and were slow to come to terms with the new reality.

The dangers ahead

It is hard to argue that the Arab spring has not been a positive event. The dangers of stagnation in the Arab world are many and its consequences include violence, extremism, corruption and the continued decline of the state. However, arguments in support of the 'stability first' theory outlined above continue to be heard both inside and outside the region.

These arguments suggest that the removal of the Arab regimes will open the door to clerical rule, chaos and further chaos. There is some truth in this. Already it is clear that religious parties have made gains in post-revolutionary elections in Tunisia and Egypt. Interestingly, Al-Nour, a Salafist party, has shown signs that it could be a political contender in Egypt. In Egypt and Tunisia it will be interesting to see how Islamic parties cope with the reality of governance after years of opposition.

The response to the Islamists' success in the West and among Arab secularists has been inevitable. There is already debate that countries ruled by Islamic parties will be hostile to Israel and discriminatory towards minorities and women. However, secularists and the West need to learn to deal with this reality. In many ways the threat to democracy does not come from Islamists themselves, but rather from secularists and the West who may seek to intervene in governments if they dislike their ideology.

One of the more curious consequences of the Arab spring has been the damage it has inflicted on al-Qaeda, a group with roots in autocratic Arab regimes. Ayman Zawahiri was arrested and tortured following the assassination of President Anwar Sadat of Egypt, and this experience played a role in formulating his hatred of Arab regimes and their Western supporters. Other affiliates of al-Qaeda were inspired by hatred of their governments, which they saw as corrupt and unfair.

The removal of these regimes and the manner in which they were removed is ultimately a blow to al-Qaeda and its ideology. For the past two decades, al-Qaeda has argued that the only way to overthrow Arab regimes is violently. The peaceful demonstrations in Egypt and Tunisia quickly proved this strategy ineffective. Moreover, the Arab spring has rebranded Arab political culture. If the first Arab decade of the 21st century was defined by al-Qaeda, the second certainly nurtured the spirit of peaceful revolution.

Although al-Qaeda has largely been discredited for the time being, instability in states such as Libya and Syria has provided an opportunity for al-Qaeda and other extremist groups. If the Syrian regime's violent repression of protests continues, elements in the opposition are likely to be radicalised and may become susceptible to al-Qaeda's ideology. As the situation becomes more violent, there are signs that this radicalisation is taking place.

The consequences of foreign intervention in the uprisings are potentially severe. In Libya, NATO support for the opposition has posed problems. Although the intervention enabled the opposition to defeat the Qaddafi regime, it has now given NATO a foothold in North Africa. Western involvement in Arab countries should be treated with scepticism, as the West's goals can be cynical and self-interested. Is NATO genuinely interested in securing democracy in Libya, or does it seek to manage the country and ensure that its own geopolitical interests are secured? It is too early to answer this question, but opposition groups should be wary of Western involvement.

Regional powers such as Turkey, Iran and Israel may seek to take advantage of instability caused by the Arab spring. Iran is trying to capitalise on the GCC's support for Bahrain following protests against the Khalifa family in March 2011. It aims to portray the entry of GCC forces into Bahrain as an occupation and is trying to build a relationship with the Gulf's Shia inhabitants. Turkey's role in the region has become increasingly important, and the Turkish government will be concerned that the conflict in Syria does not have a more serious impact than it has already had along the border of the two countries.

Opposition movements must make sure that they don't

become local proxies of the US or regional powers. Israel and Iran are likely to try to co-opt opposition movements to ensure an outcome that suits their strategic goals. And in a period of rising tension between Iran and Israel, and between Iran and states such as Saudi Arabia, there is a risk that the Arab revolution will be used in the regional cold war.

A further challenge is that many countries in the region do not have the institutions and civil society to ensure smooth political change. The revolutions in Egypt and Tunisia are likely to be the last peaceful ones because these countries have relatively strong trade unions as well as a strong civil society and civic culture.

The absence of these institutions elsewhere means that opposition groups trying to overthrow regimes must try to manipulate older social structures, such as tribal groups, religious institutions and local identities. These structures pose a risk to the integrity of the state as they exacerbate divisions in society. This problem can be seen clearly in many Arab states. For example, at the time of writing Syria risks becoming increasingly sectarian as the country's majority Sunnis believe the Alawi (Shia) sect, from which President Assad comes, is responsible for supporting his regime and assisting the brutal repression of protests.

Libya offers another example of the relevance of non-state-related social structures. Initially, protests against the Qaddafi regime were mainly in Benghazi, reflecting the city's longstanding grudge against the regime and its strong sense of localism. The post-revolutionary political landscape in Libya has a tribal tone as many of the anti-regime militias are structured around tribal groups. These divisions may endure; the manner in which Sirte, Qaddafi's home town, was destroyed by the rebels – and Qaddafi himself executed – does not bode well for reconciliation.

The authoritarian governments that have ruled Arab countries are largely responsible for the strength of the non-state social structures. Many Arab regimes have encouraged sectarianism and tribalism in a cynical attempt at divide and rule. Tribalism is a particularly valuable structure for regimes as it strengthens a patronage network that enforces government control over society.

It is a measure of the weakness and ineffectiveness of some Arab governments that sectarian, tribal and local divisions remain so strong in supposedly modern societies. In the absence of national institutions in which all citizens can participate and expect fair treatment, it is unsurprising that individuals rely on more accommodating networks such as sect and tribe. In Yemen, for example, the state is so weak that society has largely remained tribal, this being the only structure that can provide protection and support.

The presence of these structures poses major threats to the health of Arab politics in the new revolutionary era. Perhaps the most potentially damaging phenomenon is sectarianism, which can tear society apart. The Lebanese civil war and Iraq since 2003 are examples of how horrific sectarian divisions can be. Sectarianism poses a particular risk to the integrity of society in the GCC, as the division between Sunni and Shia has been exacerbated by unrest in Bahrain and Iranian propaganda. This is a dangerous situation that must be addressed by GCC leaders and by the Bahraini government, which must avoid sectarianism and ensure that inclusive politics prevails.

Where is the Arab spring going?

It is unclear whether the Arab spring can build an inclusive democracy that is an improvement on the old regimes. As the euphoria subsides, the new leaders of Egypt, Tunisia and Libya face the difficult tasks of installing democracy and reforming struggling economies that have been underperforming for decades.

A number of hurdles will make this task more difficult. In all three countries there is a limited culture of democracy and political plurality is in its infancy. In the heat of the moment, many opposition movements have not had a chance to explain their manifesto for governance. In many cases the revolutions happened so quickly that opposition groups have yet to form themselves into political parties. This poses a problem for post-revolutionary elections in countries such as Libya, where after years of autocratic rule and sham elections there is a complete absence of political parties. As mentioned before, in many countries religious structures remain powerful and will probably fill the void created by the regime's removal. It is no surprise that religious parties have taken power in elections in Egypt and Tunisia.

In many Arab countries there remains a 'deep state' that has survived the revolution and will seek to cling to power. In Egypt, for example, the military continues to have a grip on power and the Supreme Council of the Armed Forces (SCAF) has effectively dictated the timing and nature of parliamentary and presidential elections. The military has played such an important role in post-revolutionary politics that an alternative reading of Mubarak's removal is that this was not a revolution but rather a military coup.

The military's hold on politics will impede the installation of a healthy democracy in Egypt as it is not a competent ruler of civil administrations. The violence used against protests over the parliamentary elections in November 2011 indicates the SCAF's lack of ability to cope with criticism or dissent. Moreover, the military has taken control of huge parts of the national economy – some estimates put it at around 40 per cent. Businesses owned by members of the armed forces and their relatives include beach resorts, factories and mineral water brands.[8]

The military has developed a similar role in the political economy of Egypt as its contemporaries in Pakistan and Turkey. It has used its power to ensure that businesses it controls benefit from preferential treatment. Many in Egypt allege that military-owned businesses pay no tax and can buy public land at less than the market rate. Since Mubarak was overthrown, the military has been pushing for the prosecution of civilian businessmen on grounds of corruption while military officials and their allies go untouched.

Military control of the economy and politics poses a threat to genuine reform in Egypt. Elsewhere in the Arab world the military has developed a similar role, including in Syria, Jordan and Algeria. Nonetheless, the military in Egypt is an institution that must be respected, for it is one of the only guarantors of internal and regional stability. The importance of this role is reflected in the $2bn that the US gives Egypt each year, the bulk of which goes to the military.

The dire consequences of the disbanding of the Iraqi Army in 2003 show just how important the military is in maintaining security and stability. Newly appointed or elected civilian governments should try to develop a timetable that gradually rolls back the military's involvement in politics and confines them to barracks. The recent history of Turkey and Pakistan is evidence of the dangers of a military role in politics.

The revolutions in the Arab world in the 1950s were followed by a phase of nationalism and protectionism that choked inter-Arab and foreign investment. In countries such as Egypt and Iraq, large businesses such as banks, mines and hotels were nationalised. Protectionism resulted in tariffs that, combined with increasing government bureaucracy, made foreign investment difficult.

The new governments of Egypt, Tunisia and Libya should avoid the temptations of nationalisation and protectionism at all costs – and to their credit, there is little sign of these ideas taking root in the region. The new governments should work hard to create a legal framework and sufficient transparency to encourage foreign investors. Since the beginning of the last oil boom there has been an obvious opportunity to invest the excess capital in poorer Arab economies. This opportunity has often been missed, as investors have preferred the more stable and transparent economies of Europe and the West.

So far the signs are encouraging: leaders in all three countries have indicated they are intent on encouraging and protecting investment. These new governments should aim to strengthen the rule of law, the protection of private property and transparency. They should also seek to combine the traditional conservatism of many central banks in the Arab world with the development of strong capital markets and regulations that will help the private sector receive the financing it needs.

3

ECONOMIC DIVERSIFICATION IN THE GCC: THE RENTIER STATE

D ESPITE THE ENORMOUS QUANTITIES of capital that have flowed into the Gulf region over the past decade from sales of oil and other hydrocarbons, an internationally competitive industrial base has not yet materialised in the GCC, and it is unlikely to do so in the near future. The downturn in the global economy that began in 2008 indicated how reliant the GCC economies are on oil and gas revenues and how vulnerable they are to downturns in the international hydrocarbon markets.

External hydrocarbon revenues have largely acted to dampen incentives towards productive investment. As governments face a combination of uncertainty over the rate at which hydrocarbon reserves are being depleted, a rapidly growing population (consuming ever-increasing amounts of electricity and fuel) and a growing number of jobseekers, economic diversification in the Gulf region is becoming ever more urgent.

Rentier state theory is important in understanding the problems that the GCC economies face. The term 'rentier state' was coined in 1970 by Hossein Mahdavi in reference to Iran.[1] Various definitions have been proposed, but broadly a rentier state is one in which a significant proportion of the income of the state arises not as a result of direct productive activity, but in the form of externally originating rent.[2] States that derive a significant proportion of their income in the form of rent – usually revenues that accrue from some externally scarce natural resource – have historically exhibited a number of structural, political and developmental patterns. These rents primarily accrue to the state's government, which then distributes the revenue throughout the local economy. The mechanisms used depend on the form of government, the structure of the economy and the political influence of actors within the economy.

A rentier state is therefore unique in that the government derives the majority of its income from sources external to the economy over which legislative power is exercised and then plays a distributive role by allocating this income within the local economy. The role of the state as an intermediary between – in the case of the GCC countries – the hydrocarbon sector and the rest of the economy gives rise to an economic structure in which public expenditure is of primary importance and the public sector dominates, even in liberal economic regimes. As a result the public sector becomes bloated and can create a bureaucracy that may stifle private-sector activity.

A key characteristic of rentier economies is that the usual link between productive effort and pecuniary reward is weakened.[3] Because household incomes are derived mainly through the allocation of external revenue flows by the state, the primary focus of actors in the economy is to obtain a share in these revenues, whether through employment in the public sector, distribution via the welfare state or – for entrepreneurs – through preferential treatment in the form of subsidies or grants. Examples of this are the subsidies that were given by GCC governments to inefficient agricultural sectors.

Expatriate labour also plays a large role in a classic rentier state system. The labour required to safeguard external rents, for example through maintaining pipelines, servicing machinery and so on, is provided by a small, often expatriate, minority of the population. The remainder of the population largely engages in efforts to secure a share of these rent flows.

The relationship between state and citizen is thus qualitatively different from that observed in more advanced liberal economies. Public consent is maintained via mechanisms that are quite different from those that operate when the primary function of the state is to provide the basic legal and institutional framework under which business can be conducted: private property, the rule of law and monetary administration. In contrast, many of the allocation decisions made by governments of rentier states are informed by the exigencies of maintaining the consent of the population. This gives rise to specific tendencies in government spending programmes. First, present consumption is often preferred to investment, with large amounts of money channelled to the population in the form of welfare spending. Second, where investment does occur – other than that required to maintain revenues – it is often directed towards highly visible projects such as large-scale infrastructure, prestigious buildings and military spending. Longer-term investment projects aimed at initiating self-sustaining productive output have less immediate benefits, require the diversion of resources away from current consumption and are therefore politically more difficult.[4]

These structural features often give rise to patterns of capital formation in which the standard concerns of economic development are overlooked. These include the existence of 'linkages' between different sectors of the economy, the importance of economies of scale, co-ordination to avoid duplication of projects, a consideration of the position of industries in the global economy, and the competitive advantages or disadvantages of the GCC countries. Furthermore, there is some evidence that even in profitable export sectors, efficiency is lower than in similar sectors in other parts of the world.

The problem of low rates of capital formation is compounded

by what is commonly referred to as 'Dutch disease'. This refers to the tendency of the real exchange rate to rise during oil booms, as strong demand for oil gives rise to a shift in the terms of trade. This in turn reduces the competitiveness of other industries, reinforcing dependence on oil revenues.[5]

The direct link between external rents and government expenditure means that the causal relationship between economic actions and the effect of those actions on aggregate incomes is different from that in advanced capitalist economies. Changes in the rate of growth occur not as a result of the investment decisions of entrepreneurs and the policies of the state, but rather as a function of the levels of supply and demand in global commodities markets. Levels of government expenditure are thus largely determined by conditions outside the country. While this implies that at times such as the present – when energy prices are at historically high levels – governments enjoy high revenues and are able to undertake large-scale investment projects, the converse is also the case. When commodity prices fall, leading to a reduction in export revenues, the corresponding reduction in spending has to be implemented largely in the government sector. Often it is politically more convenient to reduce expenditure on capital investment rather than current consumption, so in times of falling energy prices rentier states cut back on productive investment.

Thus one important aspect of the transformation from rentier state to an economy based on capitalist production is the creation of a stable fiscal base. This is necessary to protect government revenues from changes in international commodity prices, thus reducing the liquidity risk associated with longer-term public investment projects. This fiscal base must largely arise through the taxation of corporations and individuals. This is problematic in regions where states have traditionally assumed an allocative role and taxes have been very low or even non-existent, as in the case of most GCC countries. As a rule, populations that don't pay taxes are less likely than those that do to try to hold their government to account. The issue of fiscal stability is therefore linked to the issue of democratic representation.

Another feature of the rentier state is that the usual sequence of economic development is reversed. The commonly observed pattern is for agriculture to be augmented over time by industrial production, with a services sector developing last. In states dominated by natural endowments, a large services sector often springs up to cope with the requirements of – in the case of the Gulf – the energy export sector. Thus the transition is from an agricultural economic system to a services-based system, with industrialisation occurring later, often as part of a strategy of diversification. The existence of this services sector, funded through the revenues of external rents, has lead some authors to suggest that there is a 'rent multiplier' effect, similar to the familiar Keynesian multiplier mechanism. As hydrocarbon rents are directed into the economy in the form of salaries for public servants, investment in infrastructure and the like, they represent income for agents in the system. This income is spent on consumption, housing and other services, increasing demand in these markets and thus generating further income. The full effect on the economy of changes in the levels of external rents is thus not fully captured in the raw export figures, but it will generally be higher.[6]

A final feature of the rentier state is the problem of statistics, and there are a number of related issues with respect to standard national accounting practices. The first is published nominal figures for GDP, government revenue and exports. Because such a large proportion is made up of external rents, these figures are strongly affected by changes in international commodity prices. In the case of the GCC countries, they therefore reflect the supply of and demand for hydrocarbons rather than being a real measure of domestic productivity.

A second issue related to the measurement of GDP figures for large-scale exporters of finite natural wealth is that there is no balance-sheet counterpart to the sale price of that wealth.

A good example of this is another finite commodity: foreign exchange. If a country runs down its foreign-exchange reserves to purchase imports, or to pay off its national debt, the foreign exchange spent in the transaction is deducted from the national accounts, and inverse adjustments – for example, a reduction of the national debt – are also made accordingly. This is not the case with mineral wealth. The export proceeds are added to the asset side of the balance sheet without a corresponding deduction for mineral reserves. Thus oil and gas deposits are treated as 'manna from heaven', and are accounted for in value-added terms, in the same way as, for example, commodities that are renewable on an annual basis such as agricultural produce.

Overview of the GCC: oil dependency

The Gulf region is unique in terms of international economic development. Nowhere in the world has the transition from tradition to modernity occurred so rapidly and so dramatically. In only a few generations the GCC countries have undergone a transition from an agrarian economy to one based on hydrocarbon extraction and, increasingly, a modern services sector.

The rapidity of this economic transformation partly explains why an equivalent social transformation has not taken place. Systems of government, power structures and relationships, and patterns of distribution and consumption within the resident population have in many respects remained largely unchanged during the past few decades, despite the magnitude of the changes to the economic base.

From an external perspective, the GCC countries are in many ways exemplars of modern Western-style capitalism and consumerism. Nowhere is this more immediately obvious than in Dubai, with its burgeoning financial services sector, record-breaking skyscrapers and artificial palm-shaped holiday islands. Beneath the 21st-century surface of all GCC states, however, a deeply conservative, tribal society remains very much in control of all aspects of social, political and economic life.

The polities of the GCC thus represent a unique synthesis of the modern and the traditional. While in some GCC states visitors can go to bars, enjoy nightlife and shop in air-conditioned malls, the political structure in all states is based on traditional patterns of kinship and tribal allegiance. These familial power bases were the primary beneficiaries of the enormous revenues that arose from the exploitation of the region's oil wealth. These revenues have served to strengthen the traditional ruling elites and have allowed them to consolidate their position in the face of the forces of globalisation. The elite of the GCC countries can now associate with the global elite in terms of their lifestyle and influence based on their investments in infrastructure, cultural icons and financial institutions.

Through the allocation of oil revenues via traditional systems of patrilineage, the ruling elites were able to maintain the consent of the local population and thus could make selective decisions about which aspects of Western consumerism and culture they would accept as concomitants of integration in the wider global economic system, and which they would reject.[7]

The Gulf states now find themselves in a position in which they have access to the latest technological innovations and lifestyle choices without having experienced the upheaval of social transformation that is the usual side-effect of the transition from agrarian society to advanced industrial nation. The power of 'big capital' to weaken political structures and leave national legislatures beholden to it in globalised capitalist nations is held at bay in the Gulf states. The revenues arising from private enterprise are dwarfed by the rents controlled and allocated by the ruling elite. Furthermore, much of the non-hydrocarbon economic activity that occurs in these economies is undertaken not by foreign multinational firms but by local businesses, often controlled by or in some way attached to members of the ruling class.[8]

It is clear, then, how the confluence of a traditional tribal society and enormous externally arising rents gives rise to a largely stable political structure in which the centralisation of power remains implicit. The question of economic diversification in the Gulf is thus not simply a technical exercise of adjusting structural macroeconomic policy variables. It is a more fundamental question of how to modify the structure of incentives such that it is in the interests of the population to enter into productive effort, and to what extent these adjustments will require associated changes to the political system.

An important characteristic of the Gulf economies is the existence of a two-tier social system. Large numbers of expatriate workers undertake most of the physical labour required for the upkeep of oil extraction, construction projects and all the other unskilled and semi-skilled manual work necessary to maintain the economic system. For the most part these workers come from the South Asian subcontinent, and although their wages are relatively high compared with what they would get at home, they are poorly paid and generally live in poverty. These cheap foreign workers are segregated from mainstream Gulf society and are often housed in camps outside or on the outskirts of cities.[9] In recent years, the GCC has taken steps to protect their rights, and it should be noted that if they work for government or semi-government institutions, even at lower-grade jobs, they receive the same wages as nationals.

There is another social class comprising skilled professional 'guest labour'. These workers fill technical and managerial roles in sectors such as hydrocarbons, construction and financial services. In return they receive a share of the rents controlled by the native elites in the form of generous tax-free salaries and welfare packages.

In summary, the economic system that characterises the Gulf region is one in which huge external rents are distributed via traditional tribal and kinship-based hierarchical systems, while being maintained by a large (in some countries a majority) expatriate workforce. This is divided into a skilled sector, largely a mix of Western, Arab and from all over the world, which receives incomes from the economic rents, and a much larger, unskilled, low-wage, largely South Asian sector.

A complication is the rapidly growing local population, which is problematic for several reasons. First, the general level of education of the native population has generally not kept pace with the market needs for managers and other professionals. This implies that such people will have to be 'imported' for the foreseeable future, although there are signs that several states in the region are addressing this problem by investing heavily in their education systems. Second, the relatively high levels of remuneration deter local people from taking private-sector jobs, though it cannot be long before the public sector reaches the limits of its ability to absorb new employees.

Economic diversification in the GCC states

Over the past few years, the Gulf region has consistently reported GDP growth of over 5 per cent. It has made – and to continues to make – significant progress towards the liberalisation of the ownership of capital, and in recent years has reported growth figures in the non-hydrocarbon sectors that have been above the overall rate of GDP growth. On the surface, this infers that economic growth, development and diversification are proceeding successfully. This is largely the view of international organisations such as the IMF, which in 2003 reported that 'the GCC countries are implementing policy reforms to accelerate non-oil growth and create employment opportunities for a rapidly increasing labour force in a sustained fashion, while reducing vulnerability to oil price shocks'.[10]

Beneath the surface, however, a different picture emerges. Among the non-oil sectors of the economy that are currently experiencing significant expansion are natural gas, real estate and construction, financial services and tourism.

In the expansion of production of natural gas, which is occurring in Qatar, dependence shifts from oil revenues to natural gas revenues. One revenue stream based on rents for a non-renewable resource is simply augmented by another. It is therefore impossible to regard a shift in production from oil to natural gas as 'economic diversification' in a real sense.

In construction and real estate, current activity is underpinned by the needs of an expanding local population combined with inflows of large numbers of foreign workers. The rise of states such as the UAE as international tourist destinations has further fuelled the boom in construction of hotels, shopping malls and so on. This has put upward pressure on rents and real estate prices, resulting in an enormous expansion of construction activity over the past few years. This sector must therefore be regarded as secondary in the scheme of economic diversification. A booming real estate sector may well be a symptom of a dynamic and flourishing economic system. If, however, the demand is largely from highly paid guest labour living on oil rents, or from an expanding local population that receives revenue flows via the government, there is a risk that demand for property will diminish as oil rents decrease.

Lastly, it should be noted that the Gulf region is not immune from speculation in real estate, as the experience of the 1982 Souk-al-Manakh stock market bubble shows. Even if fundamentals indicate that the conditions are right for a protracted increase in activity in the real estate and construction sectors, with the associated asset price rises that occur as this activity expands, this does not preclude the existence of speculative buying. This is illustrated by the extent to which current demand is augmented by foreign investors looking for safe havens for 'parked money' and seeking investment returns as property comes to be viewed as an asset class in its own right. Moreover, much of the real estate and construction boom has been financed by credit. As the effects of the recent financial crisis begin to be felt, sources of this credit will dry up, resulting in reduced activity and a reduction in confidence in the sector.

Another sector that has seen significant growth over the past decade is financial services. Dubai in particular has begun to market itself as the financial hub of the Middle East. Related to this is the development of the Gulf's sovereign wealth funds (SWFs), through which the GCC governments recycle their hydrocarbon revenues back into foreign financial assets. In the case of the SWFs, it can be argued that the transfer of oil revenues into external financial assets is a way of transforming the yield of one form of external rent into an asset from which another external rent is derived. There is one key difference, in that the rents from these financial assets are potentially sustainable – they have the advantage that, unlike hydrocarbon revenues, they are not directly linked to a finite resource. Nonetheless, by switching resources into external financial assets the government serves to perpetuate the existing structure of the rentier state.

The expansion of financial services in the Gulf can be viewed in a somewhat more optimistic light. The financial sector provides an essential service to the real economy via the allocation of surplus capital to deficit economic units. Thus financial services is theoretically a sustainable economic sector that can employ significant numbers of workers. The emerging status of Dubai and Qatar as regional and international financial centres can therefore be seen as a positive development. In light of the recent global economic crisis, however, it seems that a retrenchment of finance is now inevitable, with activity being scaled down throughout the world. It seems increasingly unlikely that the Gulf can remain immune to the problems faced by financial centres in other regions.

Other potential problems exist with respect to the creation of successful financial services industries. The limited human capital in the local workforce remains a significant obstacle to fully realising the potential of the sector. While expert knowledge is largely imported in the form of guest workers, the benefits of increased employment opportunities will not be available to local citizens.

Finally, what promise does tourism hold as a potential route out of oil dependency? It is relatively labour intensive and consequently could provide private-sector employment to the growing population. However, much of the work is low-paid, menial and considered demeaning. Furthermore, incomes from tourism can in some ways be regarded as quasi-rents: foreign revenue received in exchange for the use of hotel rooms and beaches. Thus the structure of the tourism industry in many ways resembles that of the wider economy. Low-paid workers provide the manual labour, while profits and rents accrue to the owners. As a result, the development of a tourism sector will not truly result in a diversified economy.

Considerations for the future

It is clear that substituting one form of rental income for another, as is largely the case with the sectors that have seen the greatest expansion in recent years in the Gulf, does little to further the goal of economic diversification. Encouraging the growth of these sectors may be politically convenient, because it does not require significant social restructuring and largely serves to reinforce existing power structures through the maintenance of rental incomes.

In the longer term, however, the creation of a viable industrial manufacturing base is crucial in any programme of economic diversification. One thing that has emerged from recent economic history is that almost without exception, the countries that have achieved self-sustaining capital accumulation are those that have been able to create successful industrial manufacturing sectors and have subsequently integrated these sectors successfully into the global economy via competitively priced exports.

The way this transition has occurred has varied across countries, and there is a continuing debate about the extent to which governments should offer protection from overseas competition to nascent industries. In almost all the recently industrialised nations, however, the transition to manufactured-goods exports started from a largely agricultural system. Much of the classical literature on the subject is an analysis of the mechanisms by which the transition from pre-capitalist agrarian socio-economic systems to modern industrial manufacturing takes place.[11]

These models are therefore not directly applicable to the GCC states. Agriculture in the Gulf has suffered since the discovery of oil. Locally produced goods have been replaced by imports, leading to the contraction of the agricultural sector. Thus any analysis of the route that the Gulf states should take out of oil dependency must consider the mechanisms by which oil rents can be invested in the economy to encourage the creation of industries that will provide employment for the increasing population, generate reasonable returns and have the potential to compete in global markets.

One important prerequisite for self-sustaining growth under a market system is infrastructure: utilities, communications, transport and power. Much of this is in already in place in the Gulf region, as successive generations of ruling elites have found it in their interests to invest heavily in such popular and publicly visible projects.

With respect to directing investment to productive sectors in the economy, the record of most GCC governments is poor. Putting aside expenditure on largely unnecessary military programmes and lavish consumption, much of the rents that have accrued from hydrocarbon revenues have been redirected to external portfolio-type investment without strategic focus. Concurrently, the availability of credit for local business has been decreasing, leading to difficulties in financing private projects that are viewed as high risk even if they are viable and important to the state.

Private enterprise in much of the Gulf region is largely sub-ordinated to the local population. There are strict rules on the foreign ownership of businesses and capital, and in many cases local entrepreneurs are required to obtain a permit to start a business. Often foreign businesses cannot be set up without a local sponsor, or are based on the foreign ownership stake being no more than 49 per cent.

Thus the process of diversification in the GCC states must be seen not only as purely economic, but also as a process of political diversification. For industrialisation to progress, there must be a transfer of power from the state to owners and managers of businesses. The role of the ruling elites must shift from the control and allocation of rents to a position closer to that of governments in more advanced economies, whose role is limited to regulator and enforcer of the rule of law. However, there is strong resistance to this in the GCC economies and the role of expatriates is fiercely debated.

The creation of a fiscal base through which the government can reduce its reliance on external revenues is an essential part of this process. This can be achieved only through taxation on incomes and businesses. This would provide up-to-date data on private-sector activities and the government could then devise ways to improve performance. Moreover, it would alter the relationship between the government and the people: as the slogan goes, 'no taxation without representation'. It therefore seems inevitable that government power will have to diminish as a necessary condition for successful diversification and free economic activities.

The transition from tribal or family-based patronage systems to broader industry-driven systems of allocation and distribution has been the subject of much debate, particularly with respect to the recently industrialised East Asian countries. One theory is that the existence of 'crony capitalism' and a failure to adhere to liberal market-based norms in these countries retards economic development and prevents a successful transition to industrialism. This view is supported by empirical evidence showing a correlation between measures of good governance and national income.[12]

The problem with the statistical correlation between good governance and income levels is that of causation: the existence of a correlation tells us nothing about the sequence of events. A more balanced view is that as economic development progresses and income rises, pressures arise that may lead to greater democratic representation.[13] The path taken by the Gulf states in terms of the political reforms that come about as an integral part of the social and economic transformation involved in economic diversification cannot therefore be determined in advance as some pre-formed set of 'good governance reforms'. Nonetheless, with states like Saudi Arabia consistently scoring poorly on such measures,[14] it is hard to see how economic diversification can occur to any significant extent in these economies without simultaneous political diversification.

Reforms will also be necessary in the Gulf states' labour markets, where segmentation causes a number of problems. First, the division between the low-paid expatriate workforce and rest of the population results in segmentation of local consumer goods markets. The bulk of hydrocarbon rents is allocated among the native population, and a large proportion of this is spent on imported luxury goods. As a result, demand for locally produced consumer goods is low, which in turn impedes the development of industry based on local markets – a key factor in the early stages of development of the East Asian states. A rationalisation of the labour market is therefore necessary in the Gulf region as part of any diversification strategy. The differentials between private- and public-sector pay need to be reduced and labour market legislation introduced to increase the rights of foreign workers.

Another problem that many Gulf economies now face is growing government expenditure and rising internal consumption of oil products. The local populations of the GCC are growing rapidly, putting increasing pressure on government expenditure as the pressure to create public-sector employment and social provision programmes increases. This pressure on fiscal expenditure has become greater following the Arab spring, as governments seek to quell discontent by boosting their spending and benefits programmes. King Abdullah's announcement of a $130bn spending programme in 2011 is a good example, and other GCC states have increased public-sector salaries.

With population growth there is a growing demand for energy, which must be provided by oil-fuelled power stations. This problem has been exacerbated by GCC government subsidies on electricity, water and petrol prices. These subsidies have not encouraged the concept of energy conservation, and as a result the per-head consumption of electricity in many GCC states is among the highest in the world. This has led many commentators to suggest that GCC states are 'cannibalising' their economic base, as an increasing amount of oil is used for energy consumption rather than being sold on the international markets. Thus GCC countries such as Saudi Arabia are losing a crucial source of revenue.

This problem will be exacerbated by a potential oversupply in the oil market. The global economy is still weak and there are some indications that economies such as China may be slowing down. This could have a serious effect on oil prices. The years of high oil prices have encouraged intense exploration and the prospect of these discoveries going into production will increase the amount of oil on the market. The development of Iraq's reserves and shale gas could also lead to further oversupply and a shift in energy markets.

Conclusion

Much of the recent development and investment that has come under the heading of 'economic diversification' in the Gulf states can more realistically be viewed as a form of 'portfolio diversification', in that much of the income that will arise as a result of these investments will be in the form of rents or quasi-rents. Also any significant reduction in dependence on hydrocarbon rents in the Gulf states must arise through a process of industrialisation and eventually integration into international markets for manufactured goods.

The Gulf economies will face significant risks as the global economy continues to falter. Weakening demand for oil will lead to a fall in energy prices, reducing revenue flows to governments in the region. Investments by SWFs in Western financial institutions and instruments are likely to have suffered significant losses, although these are difficult to estimate because of the lack of information about these funds. With credit markets likely to remain tight for the foreseeable future, external investment in the Gulf is likely to slow down.

It is critical that, given the challenges that face the economies of the Gulf region, priority is given to long-term investment projects, even if this requires politically difficult reductions in state spending elsewhere. Taking the easy route of reducing expenditure on capital formation when faced with a reduction in oil revenues will only compound current problems in the future.

★

This chapter was written during my fellowship at the Oxford Centre for Islamic Studies during 2008. I wanted to include it here in order to reiterate the importance of economic diversification in the GCC states. A modified version of this chapter has been shared and previously published in a book called *Society and Change in the Contemporary Gulf* by A.K Ramakrishnan and M.H. Ilias.

4

ECONOMIC REFORM

UNTIL LATE IN 2010, much of the Arabian Peninsula and North Africa was on course for strong economic growth. Political upheaval and soaring fuel prices have improved prospects for all the core oil exporters except Libya and Yemen, but the unrest has had the effect of worsening the outlook for energy importers. Threatened by uncontrollable civil unrest, itself fuelled by high food-price inflation and unemployment, the authorities have had to provide more generous social benefits and a 'safety net' for vulnerable groups. Energy exporters can afford such additional fiscal stimulus, but oil importers will inevitably be burdened by high debt levels and weak public finances.

The Gulf Co-operation Council (GCC) and nearby countries in both the Levant and North Africa have expanded food and fuel subsidies, raised civil service wages and pensions, and approved additional cash transfers to low-income groups as well as tax reductions to mitigate the impact of surging commodity prices, provide support for the unemployed and alleviate housing constraints. The resulting fiscal packages range widely, from 1 per cent of GDP in Egypt and Lebanon to about 22 per cent in Saudi Arabia. The kingdom is investing $130bn to finance low-cost housing

projects, salary hikes for public employees and increased spending on education and social services.[1]

Thanks to continued hydrocarbons expansion and huge
investments in infrastructure, the GCC bloc has continued
to support much of the region, with robust growth expected
at around 6–8 per cent in 2011. Despite increased spending,
buoyant oil prices (projected at $107 a barrel, up from $79 in
2010) and higher production to stabilise global supply should
underpin fiscal and external balances. The Institute of International Finance put the bloc's combined current-account surplus
at around $292bn in 2011. Thus foreign assets are projected to
rise by $195bn to $1.7trn.[2]

By contrast, growth for oil importers as a whole could average
2 per cent or even lower, down from 4.7 per cent in 2010, based
on IMF figures. Output in Egypt, Syria and Tunisia is expected
to drop in 2012. GCC countries are less vulnerable because of
their ample monetary assets, small indigenous populations and
generous welfare systems: despite unabated regional instability,
consumer spending and business investment in the Gulf continued to increase compared with 2010 and 2011. But the region's
oil exporters do face challenges, including the need to further
diversify their economies, create jobs for nationals, develop their
financial markets to support higher growth and improve the management of public resources.[3]

In recent years, the Arab region's spending on basic infrastructure has averaged 5 per cent of GDP per year, falling well short
of the 15 per cent common in other developing regions (notably
China), which gives them a comparative edge. Middle East and
North Africa (MENA) economies need to double their spending on infrastructure to 10 per cent of GDP per year (equivalent
to $75–100bn) to sustain recent growth and improve industrial
competitiveness. Arab governments have the added problem of
one of the world's largest populations of young people; infrastructure is both a requirement and a tremendous opportunity

for creating jobs and driving productivity. This is more important than any political reform in the short and medium term.

The MENA region has the world's highest rates of unemployment. More worryingly, this remains largely a 'youth phenomenon' – reported at 40 per cent in Jordan, Lebanon, Morocco and Tunisia and nearly 60 per cent in Syria and Egypt – hence the potential for further social tensions in increasingly jobless countries. The chronic regional unemployment is caused by lacklustre economic growth, the failure of most countries to develop high-tech industries, the poor quality of higher education, despite achievements in primary and secondary education enrolments, and mismatches between the supply and demand of skills.

Average annual GDP growth of 3.3 per cent over the past three decades was not enough to cope with the region's strong labour-force growth. An estimated 10 million new entrants are expected to join the labour market in the coming decade. Moreover, there is a sense that cronyism affects business opportunity and benefits only a privileged few. The protests reinforce the view that structural reforms aimed at market liberalisation and greater efficiency will fail unless more jobs are created and the political aspirations of the population are fulfilled.[4]

MENA countries rely on imported food, especially cereals, cooking oils and sugar. If there are further food-price spikes, they could face malnutrition, soaring import bills, higher domestic inflation and worsening fiscal balances, particularly in countries where governments subsidise food. Water availability per head – already less than a fifth of global access – is expected to decline further in the long term. Food security is, and will continue to be, an important issue for the Arab world: with global wheat stocks low and Arab countries importing one-third of the world's traded wheat, now is not the time for complacency.

Nevertheless, at a time of political change in many Arab countries and fiscal crisis in the West, the Gulf remains one of the fastest-developing areas in the world. The region's enormous wealth and vast supplies of oil and gas have changed the internal mechanisms of the Gulf states. Their exogenous rents offer the predominant source for national incomes. This phenomenon has big implications: any pressure for political change has taken a back seat when weighed against the economic success of the so-called 'rentier states'. The question today is whether this trade-off is still valid.

The problems of the rentier states

During 2011, the Gulf states spent their fossil-fuel incomes on facing down a dangerous Arab spring. The GCC countries became increasingly reliant on higher oil prices to balance their budgets. Naturally, therefore, the chief threat was lower oil prices. The ever-present possibility of an economic slowdown in Asian emerging markets, which have hitherto maintained a high demand for Gulf oil, coupled with persistent weakness in a downgraded US economy and the spread of the sovereign and financial crisis in Europe, challenged global oil markets and threatened Gulf economies.

However, evidence suggests the Gulf economies are resilient and the region will be able to weather a global slowdown, survive the effects of US policy shifts on Gulf currencies and learn lessons from the euro-zone crisis for the benefit of the long-proposed Gulf monetary union. The impact of a global economic slow-down will depend greatly on its nature, magnitude and duration. The principle channels are clear: lower oil prices are likely to follow declining global demand, while a tightening in global capital markets could easily result in higher borrowing costs, particularly for corporations in the region.

GCC economies are performing strongly. Oil prices, while off their peak, are still well above historic averages, contributing to strong fiscal and external positions. Many governments, such as Kuwait and Saudi Arabia, are using some of this fiscal space to accelerate progress in social and developmental areas and support private-sector activity. Preliminary data point to strong private-sector activity in both Qatar and the UAE. Current estimates suggest the GCC as a whole will see an acceleration in growth in 2012 compared with 2011.

With the Gulf economies looking strong, it is assumed that the region's rulers will continue to buy the support of their populations, the state will live off an income generated outside its borders and there will be no recourse to taxation. According to rentier state theory, without taxation, there will be no recourse to political representation or accountability. The first use of the term 'rentier state' dates back to Hossein Mahdavi's description of the pre-revolutionary Pahlavi government in Iran in 1970.[5] However, it was only 20 years later that economists used the theory when analysing the effects of the oil boom in the Gulf. Current thinking is that a rentier state extracts its entire national revenue, or a substantial portion thereof, from the rent of its indigenous resources – 'the gifts of nature'.

Rentier effects are not confined to oil-exporting states, and the notion of rent can be applied to revenues accrued from other strategic resources, such as access to major watercourses like the Suez Canal, overseas investment, migrant workers' remittances, transit fees or even bilateral or multilateral foreign-aid payments. When defined this way, Egypt appears to fit the description of a rentier state better than any country in the Gulf. Moreover, the theory posits that revenues accumulated from external state and non-state actors are internally generated by only a small fraction of the entire society and that, perhaps most significantly, the state is the main first-line recipient of wealth generated by 'rent', which is then expected to be widely redistributed among citizens in a truly 'allocative system'.

The often highlighted direct link between rent accrual, its distribution and political accountability is the most fundamental political aspect of the rentier theory. Many academics argue that the history of democracy has its beginnings in fiscal association, a key concept being no taxation without representation.[6] With such a description, it becomes easy to compare unfavourably the MENA and GCC regions with their Western democratic counterparts. The inevitable conclusion is that rentier states support society economically with revenue accruing from abroad, and that such states do not need to respond to society. This is simplistic. Perhaps rentierism does appear to strengthen or even perpetuate authoritarian systems of governance in the developing world, but it does not fully preclude the possibility of liberalisation.

Rentier state theory fails to address all the contributing cultural and political aspects of the Gulf states, oversimplifies local political dynamics and distorts the possible political prognosis for the region. The received wisdom is that power grows out of an ample state treasury; the state's wealth and strong financial position help facilitate its stability. Rentierists argue that there is a strong positive correlation between the actual rent and the strength of the state's authoritarian system. The notion of 'buying up' popular approval, which in turn grants legitimacy to the government, is central to this argument. Revenue from abroad might be said to improve dramatically the state's ability to buy legitimacy through allocation, and it increases government stability. The political economy of rentierism has, the argument continues, helped to strengthen authoritarianism – at least as far as the Middle East is concerned – and undermined prospects for democratisation, especially in the oil monarchies.

This argument ignores some uncomfortable realities. Governments in the Gulf have not become any more authoritarian since the emergence of oil. Indeed, there has been a considerable shift towards liberalisation across the entire Gulf.[7] Rentier state theory ignores both the positive impact of oil on civil society and the fact that it often proves to be the very cause of liberalisation. Wealthy rentier states such as Qatar, Kuwait, Bahrain, Saudi

Arabia and the UAE have ended up transforming their systems with typically allocative and distributive governance, whereby the ruling families allot their rent income to fellow citizens.

Within this framework, the notion of citizenship is a financial asset and helps create a clear distinction between the haves and have-nots in society. Citizenship is not only an effective relation between man and his homeland; it is also, or primarily, a pecuniary relation. It follows, therefore, that loyalty to the local ruling elite has become widely accepted, or at least preferred, as individuals find their personal economic interests vested directly in the state. Choosing to leave the local or national community can be easily translated into tangible financial loss, and it is for this reason that political dissent is rare.

Rentier state theorists see rebellion and revolution as less likely because of what they regard as an equation between the interests of the state and the interests of citizens. People would rather strive for prosperity than engage in political change. The ability of the state to placate influential social groups by paying them off with oil revenues should allow governments to survive long after they otherwise would. The distribution of oil revenues via an extensive welfare state is also being used as a tool for policing. Those who oppose the ruling elite may be denied state benefits through deportation or denationalisation. Securing popular endorsement through the efficient allocation of oil revenues may well help the state maintain stability, but it undoubtedly does not assure the total or even probable absence of revolution.

The Gulf has recently seen an unprecedented move towards liberalisation in social and political life. Although the extent and inherent meaning of this are disputed, the fact that a move away from austere authoritarianism has taken off proves the limitations of the rentier theory. Most rentier theorists argue that such shifts come about only in times of economic crisis and remain temporary measures that secure legitimacy for the regime but do not change overall political structures in the long term. But the recent liberalisation projects of Qatar, Kuwait, Bahrain and even, to a degree, Saudi Arabia contradict this theory. Indeed, there is little actual correlation between the fluctuation of oil prices and the process of Gulf liberalisation.[8, 9]

The majority of GCC states have not experienced any major economic downturn, yet they continue to encourage a significant degree of political change. The fact that this development originated at the top of the political system and is largely instigated by the ruling families themselves demonstrates the shortcomings of the rentier state theory, which sees no incentive for governments to encourage political liberalisation in boom times or periods of relative stability.

Oil revenues have made governments 'absolutely independent' internally and yet, despite local political apathy and a lack of widespread popular demand for democratisation, they continue to liberalise. It seems clear that even those who wish to see complete political change in the Gulf should push hard for economic development, diversification and reform to continue apace. Political change has come as a result of economic strength, and there is no reason to doubt that this phenomenon will continue should local governments continue to focus on growth.

The development of a knowledge sector

In recent years, the 'knowledge economy' concept has become an essential part of the Gulf states' strategic vision and plans for economic diversification. Generating broad interest domestically and internationally, questions are raised regularly as to how the region is faring in its attempted transition to a knowledge economy. Access to and the acquisition of technological and industrial innovation has always been the great divider in the MENA region. Building knowledge-based economies may well be crucial in accelerating flows of information, knowledge and capital in the global economy, but it also involves moving from reliance on physical capital and low-cost labour towards using technology as a generator of value-added exports and new knowledge-based jobs. The goal is to produce well-educated and qualified workforces able to compete in international labour markets. This is necessary for alleviating pressing problems of unemployment and underemployment and transforming comparative advantage – based on oil and gas – into competitive advantage.

As high-income developing states, the Gulf countries have major advantages over their counterparts in the MENA region. Eye-catching hubs of agglomeration for knowledge-intensive goods and services and industry-university collaboration have emerged in Qatar, the UAE and most recently Saudi Arabia. In 2009, the launch of the Masdar Institute of Science and Technology and the King Abdullah University of Science and Technology put the Gulf firmly on the map of global higher educational institutions. Elsewhere, initiatives such as the Ras Laffan Industrial City in Qatar and Knowledge Oasis Muscat have emerged as regional centres for technology-oriented businesses. Existing entities such as Sabic (Saudi Basic Industries Corporation) and the Kuwait Petroleum Corporation have developed indigenous research centres that contribute to the value chain in new and innovative ways.

Yet at present these remain largely enclaves of knowledge intensity with only patchy diffusion to wider society. The large numbers of foreign (predominantly American, British or Australian) branch campuses in the Gulf suggest that the region remains a consumer, rather than producer, of knowledge. Few Gulf nationals are enrolled in these institutions and the majority of graduates return to their countries of origin following their studies. All students are expected to study in English and not Arabic – even those choosing to study law, history or religious studies. No indigenous Gulf universities featured in a global ranking of the top 500 academic institutions in 2008. Reforms to primary and secondary education have started but will take years to work through the system. While it is impressive, tangible investment in enclave-based facilities cannot by itself deliver the intangible 'revolution of the mind' that must underpin economic transformation.[10]

A complex enabling environment is needed to allow this to happen. Educational and institutional reform must be interlinked with private-sector development, the creation of appropriate legal and regulatory frameworks, and a financial system that can mobilise and channel investment to firms whose innovatory outputs may encompass a lengthy start-up phase. Two issues in particular have pivotal relevance in the Gulf: aligning standards of educational attainment with labour markets; and rebalancing the public and private sectors. Linking education to professional advancement can overcome rent-seeking patterns of behaviour embedded at many levels of the Gulf economies and complement the top-down technocratic reforms that are under way.

Above all, knowledge acquisition is a process of incremental change that will unfold across generations. Policymakers should have a realistic understanding of how long the transition might take and target commitments accordingly. In successful East Asian countries such as Japan, South Korea and Taiwan, the overhaul of economic structures began in the early 1960s and reached fruition only in the 1980s. The challenge in the coming decades will be to steadily widen the reach of the knowledge economy so that it becomes mainstream in sectors and professions hitherto little touched by change.

This survey of knowledge economies in the Gulf has pinpointed the current state of affairs as a step in a journey, and not in relation to a fixed start or end-point. Progress has been made in areas such as enclave development and attracting higher education institutions to the region. However, a politically sensitive and systemic shift towards genuinely post-oil economies is still required. Only political reform can strengthen the conditions that will allow the spread of knowledge economies, both horizontally across the economic spectrum and vertically into indicators of human capital development and achievement.

The transfer of knowledge and technology

Just 70 years ago there were only ten universities in all 22 MENA countries. By 2000 there were 140 such institutions and by 2007 their number had reached 260, two-thirds of them founded after the 1980s. Last to participate in this academic boom have been the GCC countries. Eight universities were operating in Saudi Arabia in 2003, but at least 100 universities and colleges have been created since, and the country's annual budget for higher education has reached $15bn for 23 million inhabitants. The UAE and Qatar have established 40 foreign branches of Western universities over the same period. These developments are starting to effect some surprisingly under-reported changes.

The World Economic Forum, for example, now recognises that Bahrain, the UAE, Qatar and Kuwait are among the 50 nations most ready to utilise information technology. The number of Arabic-speaking internet users grew over 2,000 per cent between 2000 and 2008, the highest rate recorded among the top ten languages on the net. The number of web pages containing Arabic content increased by nearly 70 per cent in one year, from 114 million to 189 million pages. This bodes well for a revival in the performance of the Arabic language.

However, though many Arab countries opened their academic systems to foreign and private competition after the 1980s in order to improve them, initial results have been disappointing. These were not institutions that could promise a transfer of technology homewards or drag the region into the 21st century. Recent projects in GCC countries have addressed such problems with unprecedented funding and international outreach. Over the past five years, GCC countries have spent at least $50bn a year on higher education, and have continued to fund it annually at similar levels. This reflects two main trends: the rapid growth of higher education in the Arab world over the past decade; and the emergence of the Arab Gulf as a heavyweight academic actor in the region.[11, 12, 13]

Ever since the pan-Arabism of the 1950s, the few Arab universities that existed outside the Gulf have been plagued by nationalism and geopolitics. The over-politicisation of higher education, though largely downplayed in the Arab Human Development Report of 2009, is an important aspect of the region's higher education crisis. It is no accident that during the most violent parts of the struggle in Yemen, Egypt and Tunisia in 2011, it was the university campuses that were hit hardest. Given this politicisation and the major governmental funding that sustains it, how can education reformers cope with the huge governmental stake in higher education and the concomitant constraints that governments impose? For now, in spite of reforms and privatisations, these problems have left Arab higher education in a miserable state.

Arab academic expansion in the Gulf over the past decade reflects ambitions beyond the region. It is taking place in the wider context of the opening up of a global market for higher education, and GCC countries intend to claim more than their share. And by founding world-class, top-ranking universities, Gulf political leaders seek not just to close the 'development gap' in their countries; they also explicitly intend to reverse the balance of knowledge between the West and the Middle East. Their aim is to change the Arab academic world from one of knowledge reception to one of knowledge production.

One important characteristic of the academic boom is a dual process of privatisation amid globalisation. Two-thirds (around 70) of the new universities founded in the Arab Middle East since 1993 are private, and more and more (at least 50) of them are branches of Western, mostly American, universities.[14] (In 2008, even the most state-centred country, Saudi Arabia, whose government runs eight public universities, accepted the founding on its soil of two private universities and numerous new private colleges.) Inevitably, more and more non-native staff and faculty will have to be recruited to sustain this institutional blossoming. Indeed, the idea of the Gulf becoming a new major academic player is beginning to spread throughout the Arab world, attracting faculty, students and researchers from both inside and outside the region.

Three countries with especially flourishing academic activities are Qatar, the UAE and Saudi Arabia. Each, however, has followed a distinct pattern of academic development, and they exemplify three degrees of state control over higher education. In Qatar, funding is mainly governmental, through the Qatar Foundation: since 2003, Qatar's Education City has welcomed at least eight universities (six American, two Australian), with more to come. Qatari funding tends to cover the bulk of construction costs, but foreign universities remain private institutions. In the UAE, Dubai International Academic City, established in 2007 as part of its Knowledge Village (a free-trade zone), now houses 32 branches of foreign universities from all over the world. Financial responsibility is more symmetrical, as these branches are expected to cover their own costs in what is designed as a co-investment operation. In Saudi Arabia, the King Abdullah University of Science and Technology opened in September 2009. Its $10bn endowment, which came directly from the king's purse, made it the sixth richest university in the world before it even opened.[15]

These three patterns of academic reform are either mostly market-driven (as in Dubai) or mostly state-driven (as in Saudi Arabia). And just as market-oriented reforms have certain advantages (for example, greater elasticity and adaptability), they are at the same time susceptible to weaknesses exposed by the current financial crisis – as the failure of the establishment of George Mason University in Dubai illustrates.

Despite the attention that the new projects have attracted,

higher education in the Gulf is not new.[16] State universities began to be founded in the 1960s, after the GCC countries secured independence. Their poor results in terms of manpower training led to the first wave of private universities opening in the 1990s, but the achievements of the latter were just as meagre.

Two particular circumstances, aside from the demographic realities mentioned above and the overall need of post-oil rentier economies for knowledge-based societies, underlie the post-2000 academic boom. First, 25–75 per cent of the population of the various GCC countries are foreign expatriates, an increasing proportion of whom have the wealth and the will to provide their children with high-quality national or international higher education in their host countries.[17] Second, escalating security constraints since 9/11 have impeded Arab students' mobility in the West. Many now prefer to study in their home countries.

The immediate, tangible expression of this blossoming in Arab academe is a dramatic improvement in the quality and quantity of academic offerings in the region. While many hope this boom will help to improve education, the economy and social welfare throughout the Arab world, others worry that it reflects further intrusion by the West. But the result may be the reverse: the development of local higher education may eventually result in previously mobile student populations settling in stable enclaves within the Arab Middle East, fostering a collective Arab identity. Furthermore, previous experience shows that imported knowledge, techniques and institutions can be domesticated. These phenomena, therefore, require cautious interpretation and forecasting at the geopolitical level.[18]

GCC countries are described by many as islands of wealth, stability and freedom in an ocean of turmoil – Iraq, Palestine, Lebanon – and harsh dictatorships – Syria, Yemen – even though none of the GCC countries can be considered democratic. This raises the question: how sustainable are educational reforms in these countries?

The Gulf states retain a primary interest in exercising political control over society, as well as in securing the primacy of their own citizenry vis-à-vis foreign residents. This is particularly true in politically contentious times, during which security considerations are a high priority. Thus there questions about academic freedom and quality in GCC countries: to what extent are these regimes prepared to absorb, and cope with the results of, the world-class research they are anticipating? Although excellent research can be produced under undemocratic rule, few academic disciplines can thrive under such constraints. The humanities, social sciences and liberal arts cannot be expected to develop in highly conservative and authoritarian settings – which explains the expected focus of the new curricula on the 'exact sciences' and the expected 'domestication' of the social sciences within a framework of social engineering.

While some universities may be wondering if they want to set up shop in the Gulf, there is also resentment growing within the region. Tens of thousands of new students will be populating new campuses – in effect, new public places. Worldwide experience shows that the politicisation of campuses is common, especially in contentious contexts. The new campuses could be perceived as 'run by foreigners' and 'corrupting the youth', and might become arenas of protest.

State agencies of coercion will seek to monitor and control these new concentrations of youth and the new intellectuals, again raising concerns about academic freedom. More fundamentally, the societal impact of these campuses may involve the territorialisation and legitimising of academia. If these new hubs of knowledge fulfil their promise, they will bring into play new approaches to teaching and learning and new concepts of social and gender relations, with a predictably subversive impact. It is likely, for example, that these high-quality universities will be primarily attended by female students who were formerly prevented from studying abroad by conservative norms.

GCC societies cannot remain immune to such massive imports of manpower and knowledge – and of American-style higher education generally. The solution for Qatar and the UAE has been to set up offshore campuses in remote 'education cities'. By protecting the society the institution is supposed to serve, this type of setting preserves the campus's legitimacy at the expense of its territorialisation, whereas integration into society could put that legitimacy at risk. There is thus limited room for manoeuvre with respect to these new academic policies: if they are successful, they could well threaten social stability.[19]

Even if, to a certain extent, higher education can expand while preserving the internal political order in the Gulf states, it is unlikely that the influx of new higher education venues can proceed without exacerbating the conflict between nationalism and the necessary internationalism of the projects. First, the increasing privatisation of academia could deprive the Gulf states of their usual means of control over universities. One such tool, used extensively in Saudi Arabia, is the distribution of academic posts; its elimination is sure to frustrate elements within the state apparatus. Second, the expansion of academia is contrary to the policies of nationalisation of manpower that GCC states have tried to enforce during the past decade. The scale of the projected academies exceeds by far the capacities of the local workforce, and their international scope prohibits any nationalist preference in hiring in any case. Thus the paradox and the irony: the nationalist project of fostering world-class universities in order to secure national independence has required increasing resort to foreign institutions and manpower, and hence greater dependence on foreigners.

Can the higher education project be successfully implemented despite these contradictory dynamics? At least during the first decade, the recourse to foreign faculty is likely to predominate. Academic autonomy will be achieved when local faculty can be appointed and PhD programmes have been effectively operated and doctorates awarded. The exposure of these new campuses to international faculty, then, should last at least 10–15 years. Only then will Gulf universities be able to hire the majority of their PhD faculty locally.[20]

Another concern is regional discrepancies, which may increase as a result of these new developments. Egypt, which for a long time attracted many Middle Eastern students, now faces a social, political and economic crisis resulting from the loss of competitiveness in its higher education institutions. These institutions no longer provide high-quality education and hence no longer attract foreign students – or Egyptian students, for that matter. Structural reforms and increasing privatisation seem insufficient and have come too late to restore Egypt's influence, so the flow of foreign students into the country is likely to continue to decrease.

The attractions of GCC academia may stem the brain drain that Egypt and other Middle East countries are suffering. Some 1.4 million Egyptians work in GCC countries, and Egyptian faculty run most of the numerous Arab Gulf colleges. Both the nationalisation of manpower and the high level of excellence sought in new faculty recruitment in the GCC countries will shift the movement of academics, at the expense of Egypt. Growing numbers of Egyptians may be trapped inside their own country, while only the most talented will continue to migrate to the GCC. It is a dead end for most, a brain drain of the best.[21] The future looks grim for Egypt, which with nearly 80 million inhabitants is the most populated country in the Arab world and almost its poorest. Other Arab countries are on the verge of similar crises, including Algeria, which exports half a million national workers, mostly to Europe. But Europe is increasingly closing its doors and building walls along its southern borders.

A successful knowledge revolution among the GCC countries could detach them from the rest of the Arab world in terms of academic and scientific quality, and thereby accelerate social and political crisis in the weakest countries in the region. In the worst case, the Gulf could join a North African academic buffer zone, attracting students from the south unable to reach the north and providing them with Western-style higher education. The current higher education boom in the Gulf unquestionably augurs dramatic social, economic and political changes throughout the Middle East.

The immediate question is whether this boom is economically sustainable amid the turmoil of the financial crisis. Only the most market-oriented projects are vulnerable to international economic events: although many projects in Dubai are certainly threatened, those with higher state investment face lower risks. The longer-term question is whether the academic revolution will be a force for democracy or for reaction. The search for knowledge through higher education is both an act of political faith and a new paradigm for development. For now, it is introducing strong elements of transformation into the region, which could lead to further wealth and development and might, if properly activated, serve as a means of democratisation as well.

Effective laws for the protection of property rights

In recent years, GCC governments have come to appreciate that the creation of a knowledge economy must be supported by genuine protection of intellectual property rights. In the drive to innovate and invent life-saving devices and medicines, solar technologies and water purification systems, it is necessary to meet not only regional but also global needs. Nearly all the 300 products on the World Health Organisation's Essential Drug List, which are critical to saving or improving people's lives, came from the R&D-intensive pharmaceutical industry, which depends on patent protection.

Intellectual property rights can help create and support high-paying jobs, drive economic growth and competitiveness, help consumers make educated choices about the safety and effectiveness of their purchases, and encourage entrepreneurs to keep pushing for new advances in the face of adversity. However, while much has been done to protect trademarks, copyrights and patents by law, enforcement is another matter.

In February 2010 the International Intellectual Property Alliance (IIPA) submitted a report to the US Trade Representative (USTR) recommending that Saudi Arabia be removed from the USTR's Priority Watch List for the year because of progress made on combating copyright and software piracy. The USTR did so. A year later, in February 2011, the IIPA recommended that Saudi Arabia go back on the list because of what it deemed unacceptably high piracy rates, the government's lack of progress in legalising its own software use and a general lack of deterrent enforcement actions.

Piracy rates in the kingdom remain higher than elsewhere in the Gulf for the entertainment sector (such as motion pictures and music recordings) and for the business software, entertainment software and publishing industries, as there is little or no fear of retribution. For example, Video Mesfir was a pirate operation consisting of a retail outlet and a warehouse. It was raided seven times in 2010 with the seizure of more than 100,000 pirate copies and significant amounts of reproduction equipment. Two of the cases received their first hearing in February 2010 but to date no ruling has been made.[22]

The Arabian Anti-piracy Alliance (AAA) carries out raids and enforcement activity on behalf of the motion picture, entertainment software and publishing industries. In 2010 it was involved in 175 raids and seizures of 137,179 units of pirated products, but this is just a small fraction of pirated products in the Arab market.

In the 2011 Global Software Piracy Study, published by the Business Software Alliance (BSA) and International Data Corp (IDC), Saudi Arabia had an estimated software-piracy rate of 52 per cent in 2010, up slightly from 51 per cent in 2009. Saudi piracy rates remain high compared with the US (20 per cent) and Western Europe (an average of 33 per cent). Nevertheless, the kingdom's overall piracy rate is lower than the MENA average of 58 per cent. Even after the briefest of searches, it is easy to find pirated software sold openly in commercial markets and the police have shown little interest in halting these activities. Video-game piracy is also rampant, with games imported from countries like Malaysia and sold openly in stores and malls. DVDs and music CDs tend to be available through in-store catalogues, with 'runners' dispatched off-site to obtain selected products.

Case study: Saudi Arabia

The 1989 patent law, under the jurisdiction of the King Abdul Aziz City for Science and Technology (an agency of the Ministry of Commerce and Industry), establishes proprietary rights to most products and processes sold in Saudi Arabia. The office is seriously understaffed, however, and has amassed a backlog of thousands of applications. Patent seekers are advised to apply to the GCC patent office (opened in 1998 in Riyadh), though its application and publishing fees are more than double those for Saudi patents.

Under the GCC system, a patent granted in any of the six member states (Bahrain, Kuwait, Oman, Qatar, Saudi Arabia and the UAE) is valid in all the others. To obtain a Saudi patent, an applicant must supply a one-page abstract, a background to the invention and a small collection of drawings. If an application is accepted, a patent is usually issued, valid for 15 years and renewable for five years thereafter. The patent remains valid as long as the holder makes the required annual payment to the patent office and can show within two years that the invention patented has begun to be exploited. A patent holder may file charges against any person who exploits the invention inside the kingdom without the claimant's consent. Possible remedies include compensation and fines, along with an injunction to cease infringement.

These protections fall somewhat short of the Trade-Related Aspects of Intellectual Property Rights (TRIPs) agreement of the World Trade Organisation (WTO). Indeed, inadequate patent rules were one of the obstacles to Saudi Arabia's WTO membership.[23] Moreover, since it does not adhere to any of the major international patent agreements (such as the Patent Co-operation Treaty), an application for a patent in Saudi Arabia must be applied for separately, even if it has already been granted in another country (except for GCC patents).

The Trademark Law of 1984 appears to offer protection for a trademark or service mark registered in the kingdom for up to nine years and eight months. This is renewable by application for further ten-year periods. An amendment that came into force in December 2002 theoretically provides for fines of up to SR1m and imprisonment of up to one year for trademark infringement. This sentence may be doubled for repeat offenders; however, local courts are still generally unfamiliar with the law and its application. Enforcement has been more effective at the practical level, with the Ministry of Culture and Information periodically conducting high-profile crackdowns on trademark infringements. The Saudi Arabian Standards Organisation (SASO – the government agency responsible for issuing and enforcing quality standards for goods and commodities) may pursue sellers of counterfeit goods.

Saudi copyright law covers the works of domestic and foreign authors that are published, displayed or performed for the first time in Saudi Arabia and of Saudi authors whose work is published, performed or displayed abroad for the first time. The Council of Ministers ratified a new copyright law in 2003 (implemented in March 2004) that aimed to bring the country into compliance with WTO standards for protecting intellectual property. The law covers print publications, lectures, audio recordings, visual displays and works of art, and explicitly states that computer programmes are subject to copyright.

The law now provides penalties for selling pirated materials: a fine of up to SR250,000 and imprisonment for a maximum of six months. Harsher penalties can be expected for anyone caught producing such materials. Even so, the IIPA, which criticised deficiencies in the 1990 copyright law, says the new law still fails to meet the basic minimum standards of the TRIPs agreement and fails fully to meet the standards set by the two World Intellectual Property Organisation (WIPO) 'digital' treaties. It is doubtful that maximum fines will ever be imposed, particularly in the near term. The law fails to provide sufficient protection for sound recordings in particular, according to the IIPA, which is based in the US.

Saudi Arabia's adherence to the Bern Convention and the Universal Copyrights Convention (UCC) theoretically should protect non-Saudi works first performed outside the kingdom, though copyright violations have been a major concern in recent years. Saudi Arabia was the first Gulf signatory of the 1971 Bern Convention on copyright protection, joining the agreement in December 1993. It signed the UCC at the same time and implemented its provisions in mid-1994. Any material copyrighted in a country that is a party to the UCC receives protection (at least in theory) in the kingdom. Thus the Bern Convention should offer protection for literary and artistic property, and Riyadh's signing of the Paris Convention in March 2004 should offer protection of industrial property. Most importantly, the kingdom agreed to extend these patent protections to individuals or companies from any WIPO signatory country.[24]

The need for effective institutions

The 2011 Arab revolts reflected people's anger and frustration at their treatment by predatory and dysfunctional regimes and repressive security forces. Tunisia, Egypt and Libya displaced the rulers in short order, while the drawn-out and bloody conflicts in Syria and Yemen still drag on. Some, like those in Morocco and Jordan, have led to political adjustments, but none has yet created the conditions that will allow Arab citizens to enjoy social justice and the rule of law. Nor has any yet created a framework for the inclusive economic growth that would offer young people – some two-thirds of the population and rising – the chance of a better future.

Respect for the rule of law, equality before the law, separation of powers, and equal economic and political access for all remain by and large absent from Arab political culture, which can evolve only through effective institutions such as independent courts, political parties and government departments, a growing economy, a substantial middle class and a healthy civil society. The biggest risk is that the energy unleashed in the revolts will lead to a crisis of failed expectations. This is likely unless regional governments can build institutions that will allow human and social development and create meaningful economic opportunities.

Achieving this will be a huge task, requiring an extraordinary effort by effective institutions. The World Bank estimates that to avoid still higher unemployment in the MENA region, 51 million jobs must be created by 2020 and 100 million by 2030.[25] There are currently no plans to achieve anything like this. Failure will strengthen radical forces in the region and beyond and risk triggering a crisis from the eastern Mediterranean to Central Asia. In the meantime, a large segment of the MENA population will continue to have little access not only to jobs but also to land, basic services, finance and justice. They may be further marginalised as inflationary pressures grow, depending on, among other things, trends in oil and food prices. Fiscal problems are likely to grow, particularly in Egypt, as the government and public enterprises grapple with wage and other pressures. In Tunisia, banks may face stress as second-round effects of the slowdown permeate through to businesses and investment.

The challenges for effective government institutions, therefore, are enormous. So far the benefits of growth have not been shared equitably, as illustrated by the MENA's high unemployment rates, which often hover around a quarter of any potential workforce, with even higher rates for university graduates and women, whose participation rates are among the lowest in the world.

Regional disparities are significant too. Growth has been below potential because of the lack of economic diversification and low private investment (averaging 15 per cent of GDP compared with over double this amount in East Asia). For example, a recent World Bank study recognises the increase in total factor productivity in Egypt since 2005, but finds that this is mostly explained by factor accumulation and not productivity growth. Key determinants of productivity growth are public expenditure, exports, investment and inflation, while labour productivity has been low. To attain higher growth, there is a need to move from a low-wage, low-value-added economy to a skill-intensive and technology-based one.

Effective government institutions will need to grapple with labour markets and education systems. According to the 2009 Investment Climate Assessment (ICA), high labour taxes (social contribution), rigid labour regulation and skill mismatches are among the main reasons firms do not expand employment. High labour taxes, insufficient innovation and entrepreneurship, and a lack of labour-market clearing mechanisms are major issues too. Quality of education, as illustrated by international testing mechanisms, has been compromised in striving to broaden access. This, however, would require a complete overhaul of the governance of the education system with due regard to changing the modes of learning, teacher incentive frameworks and reforming higher education systems.

Furthermore, financial and social exclusion levels are high. Access to finance is low and the social protection system is fragmented and inefficient – almost 8 per cent of GDP in the MENA region is used largely to subsidise fuel and inefficient public food-distribution systems that do not reach the poor. Trade integration and diversification, at both product and market level, are low. Most notably, trade within the region and non-oil trade with the rest of the world have been low, impeding growth and employment opportunities

Supported by public demand, authorities have a unique opportunity to address these daunting challenges and seek a break with the past – a paradigm shift that defines clearly the path of political, economic and social transformation. The pace and sequencing of reforms will need to be co-ordinated to ensure macroeconomic stability is maintained, while judging the institutional capacities for the implementation of programmes. There is a need to go beyond governments and reach out to civil society, including economic thinkers, the private sector and NGOs, and visibly demonstrate adaptability and flexibility while carefully managing expectations and risks.

5

POLITICAL REFORM

O N 17 DECEMBER 2010, Muhammad Bouazizi, a fruit seller, set fire to himself as a protest against corrupt local authorities that had unlawfully confiscated his produce. His death became a symbol for Tunisians and later for many people throughout the Arab world. His act of desperation led to a fight against corrupt regimes, unemployment and inflation. A humble street vendor had inadvertently sparked an uprising that, in the weeks and months that followed, spread to no fewer than half the countries in the Middle East and North Africa.

Hundreds of thousands of people thronged the main squares of several Arab capitals in a stunning show of defiance. Disgraced governments fell. Oppositions looked set to sweep into power. Hated regime figures scuttled offstage. Exiles have returned and political prisoners have walked free. Change has since swept through Egypt and Libya and the forces unleashed continue to rage today, most notably in Syria and Yemen.

The turmoil could eventually transform the region by tackling deep-seated problems of authoritarian rule, weak institutions and poor governance. But Bouazizi was a street vendor. For him, as for so many in the Arab world, the protest was more about the scarcity of work and the difficulty of supporting a family, the region's sluggish growth and chronic unemployment. His protest was not directly aimed at removing the region's Qaddafis or Assads. Yet it highlighted the longevity of many leaders and their families. These regimes have survived for decades during which democratic waves have rolled through East Asia, Eastern Europe, Latin America and sub-Saharan Africa. Even neighbouring Iran and Turkey have experienced political change in the same period, with a revolution and three subsequent decades of political struggle in Iran and the building of a more open and democratic system in secular Turkey.

The relative permanence of Arab regimes in the face of numerous challenges is now under scrutiny. Four decades of stability have evaporated and new elements have emerged, prompting the current revolts. It is important to recognise that few analysts explained the peculiar stability of Arab regimes in cultural terms. The literature on how Arab dictators endured does not include popular political beliefs such as how Islam is inimical to democracy or how Arab culture remains too patriarchal and traditional to support democratic change.

If anything, the concept of democracy is more popular in the Arab world now than at any time in the past 60 years. When given real electoral choices, Arabs turn out to vote in large numbers.[1] Similarly, they do not passively accept authoritarian rule. Arab autocrats were able to stay in power over the past 40 years only by brutally suppressing popular attempts to unseat them, whether motivated by political repression or high food prices. Arab citizens certainly demonstrated the desire and ability to mobilise against their governments. But those governments, before 2011, were extremely successful in co-opting and containing the population, and leading their countries to their worst performance politically and economically.

As a result, analysts have directed their attention to explaining the mechanisms that Arab states developed to weather popular dissent. Although different think-tanks have focused on various aspects, from domestic institutions to government strategies, most attribute the stability of Arab dictatorships to two common factors: the military-security complex and state control over the economy. In each of these areas assumptions were made that, though quite possibly valid in the past, were proven wrong in 2011.

As the case of Egypt has shown, political leaderships and their military and security services are not coeval or consubstantial. The assumption was not unreasonable; many Arab presidents served in the military before they took office, including Zine el-Abidine Ben Ali of Tunisia and Hosni Mubarak of Egypt. Others trained as officers in various academies around Europe, particularly Sandhurst in the UK. Many Arab heads of state are Sandhurst alumni or have trained with the British army, including the king of Bahrain, Sheikh Hamad ibn Isa al-Khalifa, King Abdullah of Jordan, the former crown prince of Kuwait, Sheikh Saad al-Abdullah al-Salim al-Sabah, the sultan of Oman, Qaboos bin Said al-Said, the emir of Qatar, Sheikh Hamad bin Khalifa al-Thani, Sheikh Hamdan Bin Rashid al-Maktoum and numerous Saudis including Prince Mutaib bin Abdullah, commander of the Saudi national guard.[2]

In the wake of the military coups of the 1950s and 1960s, led mainly by Gamal Abdel Nasser in Egypt, Arab leaders created institutions to exercise political control over their armies and, in some cases, established rival military forces to balance the army's weight. As time went by, Arab armies helped ruling regimes win their civil wars and put down uprisings. As a result, most Middle East experts came to assume that Arab armies and security services would never break with their rulers. A clan of army generals with their assumed rulers in each country became the owners of the country's future, destiny and wealth.

In my opinion this period, which ended in early 2011, was the most damaging to the Arab republics, whose people saw no hope for an end to corruption, poor governance, fragmented institutions and control of the country's resources and businesses by a few. In summary, the whole state revolved around the ruling elite and their protection.

However, the events of 2011 show that political analysts had not predicted or appreciated the various ways in which Arab armies would react to massive, peaceful protests. This oversight occurred because the role of the military in Arab politics is rarely considered. Although this was once a central feature of US polit- ical interest in the Middle East – when the military coups of the 1950s and 1960s preoccupied the academics of that era – the remarkable stability of the regimes since has led many to ignore it. Yet a preliminary review of the unfolding revolts suggests that two factors drive how Arab militaries react to public unrest: the social composition of both the regime and its military; and the level of institutionalisation and professionalism in the army.

Egypt and Tunisia, in which the military as an institution sided with the protesters, are two of the most homogeneous societies in the Arab world. Both are overwhelmingly Sunni. (The Coptic Christian minority in Egypt plays an important social role but has little political clout.) The Egyptian and Tunisian armies are rela- tively professional, and neither serves as the personal instrument of the ruler. Army leaders in both countries realised that their institutions could play an important role under a new regime and thus were willing to risk ushering out the old guard. In countries where the security services are led by and serve as the personal instruments of the ruler and his family, the armed forces have split or dissolved in the face of popular protests. In Libya and Yemen, units led by the rulers' families have supported the regime, while other units have defected to the opposition, stayed on the side- lines or just gone home.

In divided societies, where the regime represents an ethnic, sectarian, or regional minority and has built an officer corps dominated by that overrepresented minority, the armies have thus far backed their regimes. The Sunni-led security forces in Bahrain stood their ground against demonstrators to preserve the Sunni monarchy. The Jordanian army remains loyal to the monarchy despite unrest among the country's Palestinian majority. Saudi Arabia's National Guard, heavily recruited from central and western Arabian tribes, is standing by the central Arabian Al Saud regime. In each country, the logic is simple: if the regime falls and the majority takes over, the army leadership is likely to be replaced and/or prosecuted.

The Syrian army's reaction to the crisis facing the Assad regime will be an important test of this hypothesis. Members of the Assad family command important army units, and Alawites and members of other minority groups staff a good portion of the officer corps in the Sunni-majority country. If minority solidarity with the regime endures, Bashar Assad is likely to retain power. But if disaffected officers begin to see the army as an instrument of the Assad family, they could bring down the regime. Either way, once the dust settles, Middle East scholars will need to re-examine their assumptions about the relationship between Arab states and their militaries – perhaps the principal element in determining regime survival in a crisis.[3]

The reform factor

State control over the economy in the Middle East is another pillar of Arab government that appears to be crumbling. The received wisdom was that Arab states with oil reserves and revenues deployed this wealth to control the economy, building patronage networks, providing social services and directing the development of dependent private sectors. Through these funds, Arab rulers connected the interests of important constituencies to their survival and placated the rest of their citizens with handouts in times of crisis. Indeed, since the current uprisings began, only Libya among the major oil exporters (Algeria, Iraq, Kuwait,

Libya, Qatar, Saudi Arabia and the UAE) has faced a serious challenge.

Buoyed by high oil prices, the other oil exporters have been able to head off potential opposition by distributing resources through increased state salaries, higher subsidies for consumer goods, new state jobs and direct handouts to citizens. The example of the Qaddafis in Libya serves to show that oil money must be allocated properly, rather than wasted on pet projects and harebrained schemes, for it to protect a regime. The recent Arab revolts, then, would seem to validate this part of the academic theory of regime stability.[4]

Yet the 2011 revolts have called into question the economic foundations of the regime stability theory when it comes to non-oil-producing states. Although Arab rentier states have relied on their oil revenues to avoid reform, changes in the world economy and the liberalising requirements of foreign-aid donors have over the past two decades forced non-oil-producing states to modernise their economies. A number of Arab regimes, including those in Egypt, Jordan, Morocco and Tunisia, have privatised state enterprises, encouraged foreign investment, created incentives to kick-start the private sector, and cut subsidies and state expenditure that previously consumed government budgets. But these overdue reforms were not well-managed enough to create free economic activities producing real economic growth and job creation. They were tainted by corrupt practices, such as selling state enterprises at a hefty price to people connected to the regime.

Such economic reforms exacerbated inequalities and made life more difficult for the poor. But they also opened up new opportunities for local entrepreneurs and allowed the upper classes to enjoy greater consumer choice through liberalised trade regimes. Some Middle East specialists thought that liberalisation could establish new bases of support for Arab authoritarians and encourage the economic growth necessary to grapple with the challenges of growing populations, just as economic reforms in Turkey have led to greater support for the ruling Justice and Development Party. Meanwhile, Western governments pushed the idea that economic reform represented a step towards political reform.

However, the economic reforms backfired on the governments that embraced them most fully: those of Egypt and Tunisia. Although both countries had achieved decent economic growth rates and received praise from the IMF as recently as 2010, politically driven privatisations did not enhance the stability of their regimes. Instead, they created a new class of extremely wealthy entrepreneurs, including members of the presidents' families, which became the targets of popular anger. And the assumption that these beneficiaries of economic reform would support the authoritarian regimes proved chimerical. The state-bred tycoons either fled or were unable to stop events and ended up in post-revolutionary prisons. The upper-middle class did not demonstrate in favour of Bin Ali or Mubarak. Indeed, some members became revolutionary leaders themselves.

It is supremely ironic that the face of the Egyptian revolt was Wael Ghonim, an Egyptian Google executive. He is exactly the kind of person who was poised to succeed in the Egypt of Mubarak: bilingual, educated at the American University of Cairo and at home in the global business world. Yet he risked his future and life to organise the 'We are all Khalid Said' Facebook page,[5] in memory of a man beaten to death by Egyptian police, which helped mobilise Egyptians against the regime. For Ghonim and many others in similar economic circumstances, political freedom outweighed monetary opportunity.

Seeing what happened in Egypt and Tunisia, other Arab leaders rushed to placate their citizens by raising state salaries, cancelling planned subsidy cuts and increasing the number of state jobs. In Saudi Arabia, for example, in February and March 2011, King Abdullah announced new spending plans of more than

$100bn. The Saudis have the oil money to fulfil such pledges. In non-oil-producing states, such as Jordan, which halted its march down the road of economic reform once the trouble began, governments may not have the money to maintain the old social contract whereby the state provided basic economic security in exchange for loyalty. Newly liberated Egypt and Tunisia are also confronting their inherited economic woes. Empowered electorates will demand a redistribution of wealth that the governments do not have and a renegotiation of the old social contract that they cannot fund.

Many Middle East analysts recognised that the neoliberal economic programmes were causing political problems for Arab governments, but few foresaw their regime-shaking consequences. Academics overestimated both the ameliorating effect of the economic growth introduced by the reforms and the political clout of those who were benefiting from such policies. As a result, they underestimated the popular revulsion to the corruption and crony privatisation that accompanied the reforms. Oil wealth remains a fairly reliable tool for ensuring regime stability, at least when oil prices are high. Yet focused as they were on how Arab regimes achieved stability through oil riches, it was easy for observers to miss the destabilising effects of poorly implemented liberal economic policies in the Arab world.

A new philosophy?

It is no coincidence that major political upheavals occurred across the Arab world simultaneously. Arab activists and intellectuals carefully followed the protests of Iran's 2009 Green Movement, which was bloodily suppressed by the regime, but no Arabs took to the streets in emulation of their Iranian neighbours. Yet in January 2011, the Arab world was engulfed in revolts. If any doubts remain that Arabs retain a sense of common political identity despite living in 20 different states, the events of that year should allay them. Such strong pan-Arab sentiments are forming a new political reality. Much of the work on Arab politics in previous generations focused on Arab nationalism and pan-Arabism – the ability of Arab leaders to mobilise political support across state borders based on the idea that all Arabs share a common political identity and fate.

Yet following the collapse of the political union between Egypt, Syria and Yemen in 1961 (the so-called United Arab States), it was assumed that the cross-border appeal of Arab identity had waned, especially following the Arab defeat in the 1967 war with Israel and the death of Nasser. Egypt and Jordan had signed treaties with Israel, and the Palestinians and Syria had engaged in direct negotiations with Israel, breaking a cardinal taboo of pan-Arabism. The US-led war with Iraq in the early 1990s and the 2003 invasion and subsequent occupation of the country aroused opposition in the Arab world but did not destabilise the governments that co-operated with US military plans – a sign of waning pan-Arabism as much as of government immunity to popular sentiment. It seemed that Arab states had become strong enough (with some exceptions, such as Lebanon and post-Saddam Iraq) to fend off ideological pressures from across their borders.

But pan-Arabism wasn't dead, it was merely dormant. Although the events of 2011 demonstrate the continued importance of Arab identity, pan-Arabism has taken a very different form from that seen half a century ago in Nasser's Egypt. Nasser, a charismatic leader with a powerful government, promoted popular ideas and drove events in other countries using the new technology of his day, the transistor radio, to call on Arabs to oppose their own governments and follow him. Now, the leaderless quality of the popular mobilisations in Egypt and Tunisia seems to have made them sources of inspiration across the Arab world.

In recent decades Arab leaders, most notably Saddam Hussein during the Gulf War, have attempted to assume Nasser's mantle and spark popular Arab movements. Even Ayatollah Ruhollah Khomeini – an Iranian, not an Arab – appealed to Islam to mobil-ise Arabs behind his banner.[6] All these attempts failed. When the people of Tunisia and then Egypt overthrew their corrupt dicta-tors, however, other Arabs found they could identify with them. The fact that these revolts succeeded gave hope to other Arabs that they could do the same. The common enemy of the 2011 Arab revolts was not colonialism, Western powers or Israel, but the Arab rulers themselves.

Unlike its predecessor, the new pan-Arabism does not appear to challenge the regional map. Arabs are not demonstrating to dissolve their states into one Arab entity; their agendas are almost exclusively domestic. But the revolts have shown that what happens in one Arab state can affect others in unanticipated and powerful ways. As a result, politicians can no longer approach countries on a case-by-case basis. The US will have a hard time supporting democracy in one Arab country while standing by with other allies. The new pan-Arabism will eventually bring the issue of Arab–Israeli peace back to the fore.

Although none of the 2011 Arab revolts occurred in the name of the Palestinians, democratic Arab regimes will have to reflect popular opinion of Israel, which remains extremely criti-cal. Public opinion of the US is influenced by Arabs' views on the Israeli–Palestinian conflict as much as by US actions in other Arab countries. As a result, the US will need to reactivate Israeli–Palestinian peace talks to anticipate the demands of Arab publics across the Middle East. As theories are shredded by events on the ground, it is useful to recall that the Arab revolts resulted not from policy decisions taken in Washington or any other foreign capital but from indigenous economic, political and social factors whose dynamics were extremely hard to forecast.

Patronage systems and accountable government

The last time there was such hope for change in the MENA region was in Lebanon in 2005. But six years later, the forces that triumphed in what was then fancifully dubbed the Cedar Revolution are in disarray. Lebanon continues to be racked by sectarianism, corruption, insecurity stemming from a weak central state, foreign meddling and armed party militias. But it differs from other Arab countries. Its messy pluralism does not fit the mould of patriarchal police states that took hold in the region in the 1950s, a time of military coups and oil wealth. Still, Lebanon's fizzled revolution, like those of Algeria's Islamists in 1991 and Iran's Green movement in 2009, should serve as a cautionary tale for people who see in the current Arab spring a transformation as inexorable as the changing of the seasons.

Perhaps with time Arab regimes will indeed head the way of Egypt and Tunisia, or at any rate feel obliged to surrender big chunks of power to their people as a price for survival. The sense of having reached a watershed runs deep among Arabs, particularly the young. For weeks in February and March 2011 the ubiquitous Al Jazeera channel flashed a slick montage of images between hourly news bulletins showing beleaguered autocrats succumbing to popular outrage and ending with captions such as 'Who's Next?'.

Yet for all their drama, and despite the satisfaction of seeing hated rulers fall, the revolutions in Egypt and Tunisia have had to struggle to maintain momentum. The bloodier would-be revolutions in Syria and Yemen have dragged on for months, generating ever more destruction, with no resolution in sight. Other Arab states, especially the monarchies, have so far parried calls for change with seeming success, using the familiar mix of coercion, co-option and promises. So the pertinent question is perhaps not so much who will be next to fall, but rather what follows?

The answer is not at all clear. The universal inclination of revolutionary ferment is to create a more open, pluralist, democratic society like those that have emerged in much of the world. But after two generations in a political deep freeze, Arabs face special challenges in achieving this. Among these are such essential questions as how to frame relations between Islam and the state, how to incorporate ethnic and religious minorities, and how to share revenues. Many Arab countries also face burdensome administrative legacies. Years of unaccountable rule have left hugely swollen, often venal bureaucracies, creaky courts, nasty security services spoiled by privilege, and publics addicted to unsustainable subsidies for such things as food and energy.

Other places have faced similar difficulties, but usually in a more helpful context. When the iron curtain fell in 1989 it brought down a whole ideological construct, leaving relatively clear ground on which to build something new. The well-tested, culturally affinitive models offered by neighbouring states accelerated domino-tipping waves of change in southern Europe in the 1970s and in Latin America in the 1980s. Democratic transitions in Portugal or Argentina could borrow solutions that were essentially off-the-shelf. Many non-Arab, Muslim-majority countries, including Turkey, Indonesia, Malaysia and Bangladesh, have found their own unique ways forward. But their experiences, which often benefited from such things as high literacy rates and an absence of external threats, are even less familiar to most Arabs than those of western Europe. Today's Arab revolutionaries are proud, prickly and wary of foreign influence. They will have to forge their own paths towards democracy because, as yet, no specifically Arab model has emerged.

The most obvious casualties of the Arab awakening have, so far, been heads of state. Those of Tunisia and Egypt were taken by surprise. They were betrayed, ironically, by the professionalism of the institutions intended to protect them. Their first tier of defence, the feared police, collapsed, and then the armies refused to shoot their own people. By contrast, the clan-based regimes of Libya, Yemen and Syria are hardened by a ruthless, loyal core and ringed by elaborately layered security services designed to keep each other in check and to neutralise threats by remaining shadowy and capricious. Where dictators thought they could get ahead of the curve with small concessions and mean threats, they have instead found themselves slipping violently under it.

Yet the fall of dictators represents only part of a longer process in which the unspoken aim is to alter radically the balance of power between citizens and their states. Some Arab regimes may well survive this transition, so long as they understand that something fundamental has to change. Such understanding does not come easily, as the revolutionaries of Egypt and Tunisia, the front-running reformers, have found to their dismay.

Months after the giant street protests that shook central Tunis and Cairo, both cities were witnessing periodic shows of mass people power. On 8 July 2011, hundreds of thousands of Egyptians again filled Tahrir Square, and a fervent few have camped there since then. The immediate catalysts for these protests differ, and in the new atmosphere of freedom in both countries the demands that are voiced vary widely. But their overall intent is the same. The protesters mean to signal sharp dissatisfaction with the depth and pace of change, and to remind the older men who still hold the reins of power that the public will consider them guilty of backsliding from revolutionary aims until they prove themselves innocent.

The generals who now ostensibly rule Egypt and its vast, lumbering administrative machine are products of six decades of autocratic rule. So is the elite that continues to dominate Tunisia. Even with the best of intentions these old guards find it hard to absorb the challenge presented by a newly empowered citizenry, backed by a feisty press and the streetwise zeal of bold young revolutionaries.

These contrasts are starkest in Egypt. The Supreme Council of the Armed Forces, a body of 19 generals that serves as a temporary executive branch, often seems bewildered by the demands besieging it. The generals have tried to be accessible via a Face-book page and meetings with critics. But their communiqués are woolly or bullying, and their 'dialogues' sound more like sermons. The council's decisions reflect a faintly alarming mix of deep conservatism and hypersensitivity. After nationalist rum-blings, for instance, the army vetoed help from the IMF and the World Bank, despite the offer of unprecedentedly lenient terms and the urgent need to kick-start Egypt's stalling economy.[7]

Haphazard attempts to prosecute crimes committed under the pre-revolutionary regime have generated further discomfort. Judges have passed draconian sentences for minor cases of cor-ruption and abuse of power, frightening much of a business class that almost universally submitted during Mubarak's long reign to rapacious demands for bribes. Mubarak has now been sentenced, but so far Egypt's courts have largely shielded major offenders from punishment, including the security officers responsible for widespread torture as well as the killing of hundreds of people during the revolution. 'In 1952 we had a coup that turned into a revolution,' grumbles a young activist in Cairo, referring to the army putsch that overthrew King Farouk and then replaced his liberal democracy with a socialist dictatorship. 'This time we seem to have had a revolution that turned into a coup.'[8]

In Egypt and Tunisia a sort of rolling dialogue unfolded before elections were held – public anger built up at the lack of progress, resulting in protests that prompted interim governments to make further concessions. Such protests increasingly lacked focus, reflecting an explosion of political activism. The frag-mentation alarmed liberal secularists, who feared that Islamists, reputedly more disciplined and also armed with a more populist message, would exploit such advantages and surge ahead at the polls. Their fears were confirmed when the Muslim Brotherhood in Egypt and the Nahda in Tunisia emerged with the biggest parliamentary quotas.

Salafist groups in Egypt, which represent the ultra-puritan

part of a broad Islamist spectrum and include those that once espoused armed *jihad*, have formed at least four separate parties. The Salafists have clashed bitterly not only with secular parties, but also with the declining, though still influential, Sufi groups, which represent a more esoteric and traditional version of Islam. The Muslim Brotherhood, milder than the Salafists but with pretensions to represent orthodoxy, has itself spun off new political trends. The group's rigid hierarchy and seeming eagerness to curry favour with Egypt's ruling generals have alienated some of its younger members, prompting the creation of a number of splinter parties.

In both countries, frustration at the unsteady direction of change has tended, perhaps unfairly, to overshadow real gains. Despite pressures from the army, Egypt's independent press remains determinedly outspoken. The caretaker prime ministers are broadly popular and generally regarded as committed to reform. Both countries have seen rises in crime after the collapse of the police, yet remain safer than many Western countries. Secret police services still seem to exercise shadowy influence, yet in neither country is there any sign of their regaining power.

Sparring between secularists and Islamists, left and right, has marred the emerging debates over the new constitutions that both countries hope to draft. Yet these constitutional debates are growing more serious, and on most issues a surprising degree of consensus has emerged. Legislatures should be strong; executive powers limited; judiciaries independent; public freedoms and human rights guaranteed; and social policies equitable. On the question of Islam and the state, the likely outcome may be a muddying of the waters, with the state described as 'civil' rather than secular, and Islamic law being accepted as an underlying principle for legislation rather than a literal prescription.

As the revolutionary duo wend their way to democracy, another country may be stealing a march on them. Spooked by the revolutions, pushed by a burgeoning local protest movement and better advised than other Arab sovereigns, Morocco's King Mohammed VI announced in March 2011 a series of reforms, including the drafting of the new constitution that was over-whelmingly approved in a referendum on 1 July. The king has held on to most of his privileges, and critics say he has simply bought time before another wave of pressure mounts. Yet even his modest concessions to an elected parliament acknowledge the ultimately irresistible potency of the trend towards empowering the people.

The oil-rich monarchs at the other end of the region have more time. Saudi Arabia, the Arabian Peninsula's behemoth, is understandably the most alarmed about what its rulers see as a rising threat to their world. The kingdom's ageing senior princes are shocked by the abrupt fall, speeded by what they see as the West's 'betrayal', of Egypt and Tunisia's equally aged presidents. 'Basically they want the revolutions to fail,' says a Saudi dissident, who foresees a return to the regional politics of the 1960s, when Saudi Arabia sparred with revolutionary republics in what some dubbed the Arab cold war.[9] However, the Saudis were right at that time to go against the socialist revolutions that brought failed Arab republics, army rulers and defeat to the Arab world – accompanied by more than four decades of lost opportunities for their people.

The Gulf's rulers can perhaps afford to be complacent for a time. Years of high oil prices have increased national budgets considerably. With the notable exception of Bahrain, they suffer no toiling masses yearning to be free, aside from deportable foreign labourers. Yet even in the Gulf something has changed. A gap in outlook yawns between young people attuned to the world and an older generation restrained by deference to power and tradition. In 2011, even Qatar witnessed a successful boycott of the national telecoms company, Qtel, which had to change its pricing policies following a Facebook-based campaign. In a few years, some countries could find themselves surrounded by fellow Arab states whose citizens gleefully express their entitle-ment to accountable government; it might, therefore, be worth making the proactive move to share power with the people while the ruling elite has the power to do so.

Some states provide models of constitutional monarchy that could be easily applicable elsewhere. Of course, events could turn in another direction. The earlier Arab democratisers, Egypt and Tunisia, might remain unstable for years to come. They could look like Lebanon or Iraq, the best democracies the Arab world has currently, where uninspiring politics is marked by rickety compromises shadowed by the trauma of civil war. Egypt's generals could lose patience with the rowdy revolution-aries and clamp down. Bloody turmoil in places such as Syria and Yemen could persist to a degree that makes other Arabs wary of even trying for change. Such setbacks are possible, perhaps even likely. Yet the overall trend towards democratisation is no more stoppable in the Arab world than it has been elsewhere. 'You have to understand that this is not a bunch of different revolu-tions,' explains a sunken-eyed Syrian student, taking a breather in Lebanon from weeks of protest-organising in Damascus. 'This is one big revolution for all the Arabs. It will not stop until it reaches everywhere.'[10]

The role of religion

Whether it be halal fast food, eco-kosher, a cyber-fatwa, halal internet marriage services or Christian rock music, we are living in a time when many of the major religious movements are freeing themselves from their cultural moorings. The three Abrahamic religions have not lost their importance, but they have become universal and less affiliated with any one territory, and more personal and private, increasingly embodying a spiri-tual search for self-fulfilment. They are fundamentally separating from the cultures in which they developed. This helps to account

for the mosques in the Arctic Circle built in 2011, Jewish emigration to Israel from 'lost tribes' in South America and India,
and the Christian campaign for the church to be re-established
in Afghanistan.

Globalisation has increased this distancing of religion from
culture by promoting a return to the study of fundamental scrip-
tures and erecting a barrier of doctrinal purity to fend off secular
attacks. Religious advocates say that their faiths are becoming
purer as a result: returning to sacred texts is one way to speak to
the faithful outside any particular cultural context. And globalisation is the conveyer belt on which this purer religion travels.
Nevertheless, the process is far from complete and Islam and Arab
culture are so entwined – while Arab secularist models of government have been so monumentally unsuccessful – that many
governments in the West fear a new role for religion in the governments that emerge in the MENA region.[11]

In August 2011, the Turkish foreign minister, Ahmet Davutoglu, was winding up a visit to rebel-controlled Libya when
he decided to go to the central square of Benghazi, which like
its Cairene counterpart is called Tahrir, or 'liberation'. As the
crowd chanted 'Erdogan, Turkey', Davutoglu told the masses
that he brought greetings from his prime minister, Recep Tayyip
Erdogan, and said: 'We have a common future and a history.'
From North Africa to the Gulf, the region seems to be going
through a Turkish moment. In years past, Turkey's patchy
democracy was often cited to prove a negative: the Turkish
case (along with Indonesia and Malaysia, also with reservations)
showed that Islam did not pose an insuperable barrier to multiparty democracy. But nothing much flowed from that observa-
tion – until the Arab spring.

Turkey is now being studied by Arabs as a unique phenomenon: a movement of moderate Islamists, the Justice and Development (AK) Party, has overseen an economic boom, boosted the
country's standing and shown that the coming to power of pious

people need not mean a dramatic rupture in ties with the West. Whatever the flaws of the Turkish experiment, it is clearly true that Turkey under the AK Party presents a more benign picture than many of the hypothetical Arab-Islamist models feared in the West. Turkey has gained influence in the Middle East by keeping cordial ties with Iran and standing up for the Palestinians. But there is no suggestion that it will leave NATO or cut diplomatic links, however strained, with Israel. Life has been made easier for pious Muslims in ways that secular Turks dislike; but Turkey has nothing like the Iranian theocracy, let alone a clerical class that has the final say in big decisions. For Western observers of the Middle East, an evolution in a Turkish direction, towards relative political and economic freedom, would be a happier outcome than many others.[12]

However, there are many reasons to be cautious about expecting Arabs to follow Turkey's lead. Turkey's moderate Islamism did not evolve overnight. Its emergence, and taming, took a long time; it depended on many countervailing forces, including an army which was firm in its defence of a secular constitution and was strong enough, at least until recently, to deter any imposition of Islamic rule. In both Turkey and Egypt veterans of political Islam have suffered a mixture of repression and limited participation in politics – but in Egypt the repression was harsher and the opportunities to practise democracy fewer. Albeit with fits and starts, Turkey's Islamists had already learned some political lessons when they took power in 2002. And compared with many other politically active armies, Turkey's has played a disinterested role. After taking power in 1980, the army moved fairly soon to restart multiparty politics and launch a free-market experiment. It did give a sop to Islam by introducing religion in schools, but that was a modest concession, made from a position of strength.

Compared with its Arab counterparts, Turkey's secular order has deep roots, going back to the creation of a republic by

Mustafa Kemal in 1923. Modern Turkey's defining event, the defeat of a Greek expeditionary force dispatched with Western backing, was also the starting point of a ruthless reform effort, the declared aims of which included 'fighting religion' and ending the administrative backwardness of the Ottomans. For decades afterwards, the memory of this victorious moment was enough to fill secular nationalists with confidence and put pious forces on the defensive. As a largely devout Muslim nation, Turkey never ceased to produce charismatic religious leaders, but they had to adapt to the realities of a secular republic or face prison or exile. To this day Turkey's political and legal system bears the marks of years of army-guided secularism.

These days the religious teacher who wields most influence over the Turks is Fethullah Gülen, who lives in America and is at the apex of a huge conglomerate that includes NGOs, firms, newspapers and college dormitories in Turkey, as well as schools across the world. Whatever the ultimate aim of Gülen, his talk is Western-friendly: he mixes the vocabulary of Sufism with language that is broadly pro-business and pro-democracy. In contrast to many Arab Islamists, he tries to please Christians and Jews. Turkish sceptics say the Gülen movement is more fundamentalist, and less liberal, at its core than its benign external face would suggest. The fate of several journalists who have tried probing it, and found themselves prosecuted or jailed, lends weight to that belief. People who criticise the movement can face nasty smear campaigns.[13]

But followers of Gülen claim that meetings they held in the 1990s had a huge influence on Erdogan, persuading him to abandon the idea of an Islamic state. Gülen made an unusual break with the government after last year's killing of nine Turks by Israeli commandos, who swooped on a ship taking supplies to Gaza. He said it was partly the Turkish side's fault: the flotilla should not have defied Israel. Thus when Erdogan faces pressure from pious mentors, it is not to be more radical but rather the opposite.

Another feature of Turkish Islamism is the number of thriving businesses with ties to the Gülen movement. Among the drivers of Turkey's expansion – the country's GDP per head is three times that of Egypt – are provincial entrepreneurs. It is now commonplace to stress the AK Party's roots in the new Anatolian bourgeoisie and its appeal to the consumers of the country's new-found wealth: people who mix Muslim piety with a taste for expensive cars. These groups set limits to the AK Party's ambitions; like most rich folk they favour stability. In the Arab world there are middle-class Muslims who look with envy at the confidence of their Turkish counterparts.

Ibrahim Kalin, an adviser to Erdogan, posits another difference between AK and political Islam as it emerged in Egypt and Pakistan in the 20th century. Even when pretending not to, the latter movements always dreamed of a powerful Islamic government, using the tools of modern statehood, like universal education, to impose a Muslim order. AK, by contrast, lives comfortably in a world of 'lighter' states, where other agencies, including NGOs, the private sector and academia, can play a bigger role. In AK circles it is common to hear such post-modern talk mixed with nostalgia for the Ottoman era, when each faith ran its own system of education and personal law. Ali Bulac, a columnist, argues that citizens with civil disputes should consider Muslim arbitration; he says that could be combined with retaining the secular penal code, a cornerstone of the republic. Muslim democracy is already a novel creature, and is still evolving.[14]

Unfounded fear

Turkey's experience has its strengths and weaknesses as a model for the Arab world, but in any case it is important to remember that those pushing for various theocratic-democratic hybrids are in a minority. One of the most fascinating characteristics of the largest and most important of the Arab spring protests, in Egypt and Tunisia, was that the animating spirit that brought millions of ordinary Arab citizens out into the streets was not religion or any version of religious politics, but nationalism and a broad-based social consciousness. The country-specific and broader Arab nationalist sentiments that brought such huge crowds together had long been considered dead, or at least moribund, by many observers.

A few governments have tried to blame the uprisings on Islamist plots, as well as that old standby 'foreign meddling', but the symbolism and rhetoric behind the protest movements have disproved these allegations irrefutably. In Tunisia, one of the most powerful chants was '*Tunis huwa al-hal*' (Tunisia is the answer), a clear-cut retort to the Muslim Brotherhood slogan of '*Islam huwa al-hal*' (Islam is the answer).

In Egypt, a striking feature of the protests was not only their secular but also their ecumenical character, with Muslims and Christians joining and protecting each other during prayer, and the devout mingling comfortably with the sceptical. That Egyptians came together across these potential or presumed dividing lines was a clear recognition that for the society to be united, in this case against the presidency of Hosni Mubarak, it had no choice but to push religious identity to the background. In other words, the diversity of Egyptian society meant that the Islamist approach, ideology and symbolic repertoire would have been more of an obstacle to than a vehicle of success against the regime.

There is no doubt the Muslim Brotherhood participated, in some cases significantly, in the protest movements and counted on being primary beneficiaries of an opening up of Arab political space, especially through elections. The Egyptian Brotherhood, for example, was wise not to overplay its hand by thrusting itself and its ideology into the forefront of a movement for which it was not responsible and which gained power by bringing a huge number of people together across religious and other divides.

In any case, the Islamist movement is not a united one. By

staying in the background its adherents have implicitly recognised that it has deep limitations when an entire society needs to be mobilised – in this case for the purposes of overthrowing the government. That means the same limitations apply any time an Arab society needs to be successfully mobilised, although this obvious point will probably remain largely unarticulated. So while Islamists may be looking forward to trying to exploit new Arab political openness, they must have noted with dismay that it was not their ideology but a secular and ecumenical nationalism that animated the most important of the Arab revolts.

The Bahraini case also demonstrates the dangers of Arab sectarianism and the need to move quickly towards a secular order in which the state is neutral on matters of religion, and religious constituencies are treated equally by the government. In Egypt, the secular and ecumenical nature of the protests was a major factor in their size, power and success, whereas in Bahrain sectarian divisions are at the heart of government instability and the anger of the disempowered.

Commenting on the heterogeneous nature of their societies, some Arab analysts write openly that only a secular approach involving government neutrality on religious matters can have any chance of producing fairness and equality. Most Arab societies are strikingly heterogeneous, in many cases a mosaic of sectarian, cultural, ethnic and other diversity. Whether in Bahrain, Yemen, Iraq, Syria, Egypt or Libya, secular governance may express the legitimate rights of a majority while successfully protecting the rights of minorities and individual citizens.

Even though they have not been at the forefront of the most important Arab protest movements, Islamists are no doubt waiting on the sidelines, hoping and preparing to benefit from new political space. But the new Arab order, especially since it is being born in such a strikingly secular and ecumenical spirit, and whether secular or Islamic in character, must secure freedom, good governance, equity and human rights for all its people.

Otherwise, as the Iranian experience shows, it will only set the stage for more oppression, division, economic failure and civil conflict in the not so distant future.

6

CONCLUSION:
A MANIFESTO FOR CHANGE

HISTORY WILL REMEMBER the year 2011 as one
of incredible change in the Arab world. The status
quo has been irreversibly destroyed and an era of docile
populations, and the Arab 'regime system' that extended
from North Africa to the Gulf, is changing. Governments
can no longer be secure in believing they can dictate their
wishes and stick with the old model of governing. As I write,
during the second quarter of 2012, I see an Arab world that
finds itself nervously entering a new era, dealing with a loss
of control, anarchy and daily massacres, while rulers fret
about their futures and wonder whether they have done
enough to pacify their people.

This is one of the most exciting times to be an Arab.
The past 60 years, especially in North Africa and the Levant,
have been the worst in our history, after British and French
rule. The wave of change has brought an end to pan-Arab
nationalism, which brought to power military leaders who
enforced their rule through ironclad security and achieved
only military, economic and social failures.

The opportunities that present themselves now are vast.
For the first time in decades Arabs are rediscovering political
discourse, and it is a pleasure to witness. The solidarity with

··· 93 ···

the Arab spring expressed in other countries is heartening. Media coverage of Arabs demonstrating in capitals across the region has improved their image internationally. In the first decade of this century, unfortunately, Arab nations suffered fallout from the horror of the 11 September 2001 attacks in the US. In the second decade, Arabs will be associated with freedom and bravery in the face of tyranny within. In my view, if many Arab nations had had the self-respect of governing themselves, their response to the 9/11 disaster would have been clearer and more transparent. But some regimes lacked the legitimacy to defend themselves against unfair propaganda, especially from the US, who found it easy to label a nation 'terrorist' when its interests dictated.

What is clear is that life for politicians across the spectrum is not going to be easy. Regardless of whether governments are democratic or not, they are going to face huge challenges. Population growth, unemployment, badly performing economies, a highly connected world and security and environmental problems will pose serious challenges in the coming decades. New governments in Egypt, Libya, Yemen and Tunisia will have to work hard to establish their credibility and meet the high expectations of their people. The governments that survived the Arab spring will exist uneasily while their citizens observe how the 'new democracies' of Egypt and Tunisia are progressing.

Unless governments can deal with these challenges, it will be hard to improve the lives of ordinary people across the region who currently have high expectations. Many Arabs are more interested in their daily conditions than in the grand ideas of democracy and politics. For them, employment and economic considerations are paramount.

However, it would be foolish to underestimate the politicisation of ordinary Arabs at this juncture. Arab governments should realise they must work harder to reform their institutions and make sure that their citizens are satisfied.

Political reform

How can reform be achieved in real terms and in a manner suitable for our culture and religion?

First, Islam provides ethics and morals that we should use in our system of governance. For the Arab spring to be successful there must be unity among Arab leaders. They should take inspiration from the Koran and the sayings of the Prophet Mohammed that leaders should be just and fair in their manner of governance. It is sad that since the revolutions of the 1950s Arab governments have failed to act in a just and fair manner. Leaders should remember that God is watching them and is the regulator of their actions and deeds.

Many Arab states have lost their ideological direction. Following the revolutions of the 1950s, the ideologies of socialism and Arab nationalism were used to shape the foundations of the new Arab states, but in reality these principles were not applied to governance.

The absence of ideological and moral direction from Arab leaders has led to problems within the societies they govern. There is a lack of self-esteem, confidence and civic pride among many Arabs. Corruption is common in all sectors of society, including among politicians and their families. Perhaps the most serious problem is that the absence of sound ideology from the state has led to the rise of extremist groups such as al-Qaeda. Arab governments should address this and rediscover the guidance that is provided for them in the Koran. Arabs and Muslims have much in common and political thought should encompass this, bearing in mind the concept of the *Ummah*, the global community of Muslims.

Arab leaders need to embrace relevant, fair and just constitutions. Within the constitution they should build strong institutions such as parliaments, a legal system and militaries that are separated from the political sphere.

According to Francis Fukuyama's latest book, *The Origins of*

Political Order, a successful modern liberal democracy combines three principles within its institutions: a strong state; the state's subordination to the rule of law; and government accountability to all its citizens. According to Fukuyama, democracy will not succeed unless it applies these principles to its style of management and strikes a good balance between them. Applying these principles to Arab states is not an easy task, but Arab leaders should attempt it. From what we can see, political Islam or Islamists are the rising power; they should be allowed to prove themselves because of their roots in Arab nations.

Two models are in existence today. Iran, an extreme sectarian example, is run by theocrats who hide their self-interest behind the mask of the state and use a façade of theocracy to rule Iranians in the way that Arab military elites have used security as a pretext to hold on to power. This system will fail as economic problems such as inflation worsen, a young population becomes increasingly restless with the state of affairs and corruption becomes entrenched. Much of what is going on in Iran today is contrary to Islam, which places the well-being of the people and the *Ummah* at its heart.

The other model is Turkey, which strikes a balance with Islamic rule that adopts a pluralist approach and takes into account equality, democracy and the rule of law for every Turkish citizen. Turkey today under Recep Tayyip Erdogan is a secular nation ruled by an Islamic, pluralist party. The Turkish model is successful, and it is the one that new Arab democracies should learn from. What makes Turkey a success is not just its transparent democracy but also its vibrant economy, which brings the country stability and support. Any new Arab government will face huge difficulties unless it immediately puts into effect an Islamic model that is pluralist: one that is in favour of freedom and the protection of other beliefs and against sectarianism; one that grows the economy, creates jobs, and provides services and security; and one that builds effective institutions, applies the

rule of law, provides social justice and reforms education to meet
labour-market requirements.

Arab society needs to become freer. The conflict with Israel
has enabled regimes to govern with a 'security first' mandate.
This has allowed states such as Syria to keep emergency laws in
place for decades that suspend citizens' constitutional protection.

Arab leaders should address this. The media and the courts
should be independent of government. And, given greater
freedom, citizens should be able to challenge the government
and win in a court of law, especially when their property rights
are jeopardised.

At present, the institutions of civil society are viewed with
suspicion by Arab governments. Those who run them are often
harassed and their activities made harder by a state bureaucracy
that works against them. Arab leaders should make sure that civil
society is protected and supported by the state.

The combination of a free media, a strong legal framework
and civil society will provide checks and balances to protect the
system from abuse and corruption. This protection will ensure
the Arab world can liberate itself from tyranny, misgovernment
and the monopoly of resources by unaccountable elites.

Military rulers and their civilian allies are unable to cope
with the problems that Arab countries now face, and in any case
are inappropriate leaders. The leadership required now must be
sophisticated and technocratic – people who understand the realities and nuances of the 21st century.

There needs to be a universal stand against foreign intervention in Arab politics. Using democracy as a pretext to intervene
in Arab countries has been discredited after Iraq, and this lesson
cannot be forgotten. The invasion of Iraq resulted in chaos, sectarianism and the erosion of the institutions of state. The example
of Libya should not set a new precedent that Western countries
can use to justify further intervention.

Western involvement in Arab states is partly to blame for the current problems in the Arab world. Why did the West support Hosni Mubarak for so long? The security of Israel has meant that many Arab leaders get the West's approval on the basis of their docile foreign policy and commitments to Western foreign policy goals. This has been at the expense of their ability to ensure good governance and pursue the best interests of their people.

Iran is one of the biggest threats to the Gulf states. It encourages internal sectarian divisions within the GCC and has no wish or ability to co-operate with the Sunni population of the Gulf. It has an exclusive agenda to support the Shia of Iraq, Yemen, Lebanon, Syria and Bahrain. This is a strategy designed to divert attention from its internal problems: high unemployment, a failing economy and internal dissent. Today Iran has a limited space to manoeuvre in mainly spreading sectarian division in Arab countries and in developing its nuclear programme. Arab states, especially those in the Gulf, should not seek to provoke Iran. Rather, they should work to ensure that diplomatic ties remain alive. Today's Iran will, like the Soviet Union, reach the point of demise once its economy becomes totally inefficient.

Israel is a source of division within the Arab world and Arab states and people will always work to limit its power. There should be a unified diplomatic effort to ensure that Israel abides by international law, retreats from occupied Arab land and allows a thriving Palestinian state to develop. The Arab-Israeli conflict is a drain on the resources of the Arab world and this cannot be allowed to continue. It is my strong belief that once Arab nations are run by wise and capable leaders their approach to the Arab-Israeli conflict will change and reflect a meaningful, realistic approach that alters the balance of power. Once there is transparency between the people and their rulers, this conflict will be handled differently and will reflect realities on the ground. Failures will be an incentive for improvement, unlike now, when failure is treated as victory by regime-controlled media, and things go from bad to worse.

The Arab states can limit the power of Israel through a combination of diplomatic lobbying and military deterrence. The Lebanese wars with Israel have proved that it is possible to develop a relatively cost-effective military deterrent to Israel.

In terms of Arab foreign policy, Egypt needs to rediscover its role as the leading Arab state. Under Mubarak Egyptian foreign policy was muted. The signing of the Camp David agreement with Israel in 1978 resulted in a period of isolation that diminished Egypt's role in the Arab and Islamic world. Egyptian leaders should take advantage of current events to take a decisive foreign policy position that is uninfluenced by Western powers. Egypt is the key and the centre for Arab nations' strength and power. It should assume its usual role as the leader of Arab nations. We have seen that when Egypt is isolated the Arab nations become prey to division and weakness, even with Iran.

Economic reform

Economic reform is crucial in the Arab world. The state must act as a regulator and defender of stability rather than as an actor in the market competing with private-sector businesses. Meritocratic and competitive behaviour should be encouraged and monopolies banned.

The leaders of Arab republics such as Syria could not invest abroad and therefore exploited the local economy by stripping every opportunity from local businessmen. The state controlled everything and its leaders manipulated money and business, leaving people with no hope or opportunity to thrive. Corruption by the former ruling elite in Tunisia was so embedded that it left few opportunities for anyone outside Zine el-Abidine Ben Ali's ruling circle.

New Arab leaders should break up state companies and privatise them through private sales and IPOs on the stock market. The privatisation of government-owned assets has a positive effect on their efficiency and overall performance. It also allows governments to reduce budget expenditure, and thus prepares economies for the post-oil era when it will not be so easy to subsidise services. Sell-offs of utility companies also ensure that the real costs of services such as electricity and water are passed on to consumers, hopefully making them more aware of controlling their consumption. This is particularly important in the Gulf, where water and power are widely subsidised leaving citizens with little awareness of their environmental impact. When contracts are properly designed, privately run utilities also tend to invest in future capacity in a more rational manner than state-owned firms, for which profits and losses are irrelevant.

Positive social consequences can flow from privatisation when it is properly conducted. The listing of large government companies turns citizens into stakeholders in the state's economic growth. In some cases the sell-off of government assets has been described as a system of wealth redistribution. As an added bonus, in some GCC countries shareholder meetings can serve as one of the few forums in which open criticism and discussion of the management of state-linked institutions can take place.

To realise more of these potential advantages, however, and to encourage more privatisation, legal frameworks need to be improved and state assets more thoroughly prepared for sale. For privatisation to work, governments will have to reform the workforce and ensure that citizens have skills appropriate to the private sector. This will require sweeping reform of labour markets to ensure that unemployment does not threaten the progress of privatisation.

Small and medium-sized businesses (SMEs) have an important role. Their development should be sponsored by the state, which must guarantee small loans and ensure their availability. During the growth years of the past decade, banks and other financial institutions had little incentive to lend to SMEs – with their risky long-term business plans – as they could make money more quickly in real estate or other assets. Loan terms made it hard for entrepreneurs to secure financing, and many banks in the region offered few products for SMEs. Banks should pay more attention to their potential. The recession and the fall in the value of assets such as property and equities should make them realise that investment in SMEs and innovative projects is not as risky as many believe.

The Arab region has a weak base of light industry in the science and technology sectors. But it has a lot of potential: there is a concentration of capital that could be invested in these industries; the low-tax environment could be used to attract companies from outside the region; and both skilled and unskilled labour is easily available. The development of these industries could play an important role in the diversification of the region's economies and also give them a long-term advantage in the global economy.

There have been some attempts at developing infrastructure that would assist such development. In the UAE, Internet City and other free zones have been established to attract technology companies. In Abu Dhabi, Masdar, a renewable energy company, has been established with government investment with the aim of making the emirate a world leader in renewable energy. Qatar has also enjoyed at least a short-term success in recruiting partners to build itself a niche in research and development, particularly with regard to healthcare technologies.

Governments in the region should consider giving more support to such industries by creating incubators and other grants for these types of small businesses. They also need to cut costs for these businesses and set up specific units to support them. There are many Arab venture capitalists who invest in technology and scientific ventures outside the region, and policies should be adopted that encourage the relocation or development of such businesses within the region.

Arab leaders should also accept the need to create states that

can compete on the international stage and attract foreign investors. Bureaucratic procedures should be simplified, with offices
providing a 'one-stop-shop' for foreign investors to ease the
opening of new companies and other legalities.

Employment should not continue to be dominated by the
public sector; job creation in the private sector needs to be supported. The state should take responsibility for creating an education system that prepares students for private-sector jobs.

In the Gulf, governments will not be the driver of diversification. The most effective agent for economic development is
the private sector, and governments must do what they can to
support the development of world-class enterprise in the region.
To do this, the Gulf needs to build a reputation as an environment where it is easy to do business.

These are obvious steps that need to be taken, but they all
take time to implement. Nonetheless, progress is being made;
Saudi Arabia was ranked 13th in the World Bank's 2009 Doing
Business survey. Other countries in the region should seek to
emulate the kingdom's success.

Fukuyama outlines the steps necessary for reform. First, governments must support education, openness and the protection
of property rights to create the right conditions for economic
growth. Productivity must then be increased, and this will lead
to greater investment, the growth of GDP, a rise in per-head
income and a prospering nation.

GCC reform

The Gulf states have a responsibility to be role models and act
in the best interests of their people. The GCC should grasp the
opportunity to be the powerhouse driving positive change in the
Arab world, while others are in a state of disarray and regression.
Qatar was swift to show leadership in its reaction to the events
of the Arab spring, and there is no doubt that Al Jazeera played

a crucial role in bringing down Arab regimes. Moreover, we should appreciate the importance of having means available for people to communicate and co-ordinate their actions and ideas.

The GCC will require vigilant and determined leadership that will go the extra mile to improve the life of its peoples. It will require a well-co-ordinated and balanced reform plan acceptable to rulers and citizens that takes into account future needs. History has shown that change must be introduced when you are strong, not when your leadership and control is weakened. I hope people will learn from what happened to the fallen Arab leaders.

Our world is changing and people will have increasing power in the future. Arab leaders should understand that, and that in this new age of free media, with access to the internet and satellite TV they will be judged by their actions.

The GCC should become more active as a bloc, following a strategy that is accommodative and integrative with other powers and that strengthens its credibility in the international arena. That credibility will to a large extent depend on how efficiently the GCC member states act domestically, regionally and internationally and on how they act to preserve their best interests. As pressure on resources increases, the GCC must have the military capability as well as the diplomatic skills to defend its people, resources and achievements.

In order for the GCC states to be taken seriously in the future, they should devise a system that involves their people in the way they are governed without allowing it to be hijacked by sectarian or tribal agendas. 'Shura', or the process of allowing people to participate in the governing system, should be introduced effectively to ensure that the populations of the Gulf understand the responsibility that accompanies democratic participation.

Making a coordinated effort all GCC states should devise a constitution that gives rights to citizens and in which the monarchs or sheikhs play a just role. This system should be inspired by

Islamic teachings in this regard, but could be pluralist and fair and supportive of movements for a full civil society. The GCC leaders are capable of implementing a constitution in which everyone is accountable, and this can be used as a model for other Arab nations. GCC states should devise their system of governance in a way that suits their internal needs and should not feel pressured by the demands or wishes of others who wish to influence them with their agendas. There is a historic opportunity for the Gulf states to transform themselves into well-developed and innovative societies. The leaders should have the courage to act in the best interests of their countries.

The Saudis have a responsibility to represent Islam as a viable system of governance in the modern world. They need to open themselves to the challenges they face, such as the need to take steps to avoid the young becoming disaffected, to create jobs and to diversify the economy. Saudi Arabia's wealth, political power and religious significance mean that its leadership should play a leading role in the region, calming and stabilising where necessary.

The ruling elites of the GCC should be encouraged to play a more transparent role in the governance of their countries. Their privileges should be distributed in a system that is fair and meritocratic. Poor performance or wrongdoing should result in the loss of privileges.

The citizens of the Gulf need to change their perception of the role of the state. Since the discovery of oil, wealth has tended to be distributed by the state. Citizens have developed a sense of entitlement to undemanding jobs in the public sector, while business has grown accustomed to the strong growth recently experienced by the oil-producing economies. As a result, wealth has not been accumulated through hard work, experience, innovation or risk-taking. This does not encourage resilient business, value creation or contribution. GCC countries will need to address this if they are to reform their economies and encourage a more productive society.

The future

In one year, the Arab spring has achieved changes unimaginable in the previous fifty. The removal of the old regimes was necessary. If they had remained in power, the chances of violent political change, foreign intervention and instability would have increased. However, opposition movements and activists should recognise that there are huge risks ahead. Since the demise of Saddam Hussein's regime, there has been a new cold war between Saudi Arabia and Iran. The American-led war in Iraq not only killed many people and displaced millions, but also spurred anarchy, sectarian wars and divisions, and new alliances in the Arab world.

If the state institutions are not effective and not respected, the problems seen in Iraq could spread to the other Arab states following the Arab spring. If the new governments are not strong and decisive, the result may be an upsurge in corruption, foreign interference, insecurity and sectarianism.

The new Arab world should be a region in which diversity is encouraged. Religious minorities and political ideologies should be protected. Human rights, including those of the supporters of the old regimes, should be respected. Countries with diversity are proven to thrive.

Acts of peaceful protest must be allowed and have proved highly effective in the past. The Palestinian *intifada* of 1987 achieved a huge amount by attempting to adopt peaceful tactics, with violence occurring only under provocation. Governments should note that Islam provides guidance that should encourage peaceful political change. But peaceful protest counts for little in the face of the violent tactics that regimes such as Syria are using.

My hope is that the ideas in this book will help Arab leaders and their citizens take the brave steps that are needed towards implementing reform. My own experience in government has allowed me to understand the pressures and difficulties that they face, and I am sympathetic. However, there is a historic opportunity for Arabs to develop the kind of societies that they deserve, and this opportunity must not be missed.

A recent Iranian threat to close the Strait of Hormuz – a measure that could cause 35 per cent of all seaborne oil to be blocked from world markets – illustrates how bankrupt some rulers have become and why such regimes must go if their people, and other nations, are to enjoy peace and prosperity.

Egypt is likely to fall under Islamic rule but the military is likely to continue to exercise ultimate control. Tunisia could lead the way with its model provided it has early success economically and in job creation. Yemen, even when Ali Abdullah Saleh leaves, will fall into anarchy and civil war as it has all the ingredients for failure. Libya will exist in a state of tribal strife but oil wealth will calm things down, with a move towards the rule of tribes rather than institutions. Syria will collapse sooner or later, and the fall of the current Iranian regime or any domestic turmoil there would speed the fall of the Assad regime. Syria will have a chance to succeed post-Assad because of its educated population and their entrepreneurial spirit. Bahrain and Oman have more satisfactory prospects. People there should realise that the GCC states will always act as a bloc once their security is at risk. Bahrain will not be allowed to come under the control of Iran, nor will Iran be able to offer a better future to Bahrain. The regime in Bahrain must however reform, and there is no excuse for them to delay that. Without GCC support and help, especially from Saudi Arabia, Bahrain lacks the ingredients for a viable state. The rulers there should recognise this and change their attitude towards their citizens. Fair distribution of wealth, accountable government and freedom for the people to live a dignified life are the way forward.

Following the Arab spring, states that have managed to regain their freedom must address the big issue of nation building. Unfortunately, there is little sign of this happening, especially when it comes to laying out a direction for political, economic, or social change. This may be the inevitable result of long years of bad governance, outdated education systems and internal as well as external influences that disturbed the allegiances of the people. The GCC states were not immune from the influence of the Arab spring, but they have so far largely managed to ensure that the situation remains stable and calm. However, the Arab spring has shaken the old mindset and led to more dynamic forward thinking, which has encouraged a greater sense of hope among the people.

What transpired from the Arab spring is that the internal threat was potentially greater than the external threats played up by the regimes. But there is no doubt that social media and the internet, driven by external and internal forces, had a huge impact.

I strongly believe that the failures of the US in Iraq and Afghanistan have laid the ground for a future for those countries in which anarchy and sectarianism will thrive. Iraq has been destroyed as a nation. For example, before the American invasion, 3 million Christian Iraqi citizens lived in peace there; today only 500,000 remain, with many waiting for immigration permits to go to the US, Europe or Australia.

This kind of turmoil and anarchy in the Arab world may be what Israel and its allies have wished for for a long time. However, recent events in the region have made it clear that Iran will fight to keep the Syrian regime in place as it helped bring Iran's influence into the Arab world. For the Arab people, Syria was the last defender of the Arab cause to bring justice to the Palestinian people. Today, Syria's dependence on Iranian support has undermined its relationships with its Arab 'brothers', while its dark side has been exposed by killing its own people to hang on to power rather than using its well-stocked arsenal to fight Israel, as it claimed it would.

One country that understood the forces behind the Arab spring is Qatar. The leadership read the future right and by deploying its wealth, strong diplomatic power and its media flagship, Al Jazeera, Qatar filled the role traditionally taken by big countries like Egypt, Syria and Saudi Arabia.

Within the Arab world, only the GCC states have managed – and in not many years – to establish a system under which economic growth and living standards have improved. Some will argue that it is because of the oil money, but Arab countries such as Egypt, Libya and Algeria had huge oil and gas reserves.

I believe that the GCC model is a good starting point for developing a fairer and more sustainable system of governance. Politicians who embark on reform will find themselves increasingly in favour with the people they represent. Buying favour with money or privileges is not sustainable; only a system that involves fairness, transparency and the rule of law will be. One thing that we all have to realise as Arab nations is that tribal or sectarian allegiances will have a distorting and problematic impact on any conventional democratic option, and therefore a system that combines an equality of citizenship with allegiance to the state will be the best way forward. The GCC could devise a model along such lines. In the end the test will be that it is a workable system considered acceptable and fair by most citizens.

On my first business trip to Japan and South Korea in 1985, a senior Korean government official told me that it was his country's plan to compete with Japan in 10–15 years' time. I thought this was just wishful thinking but I could see the determination in his eyes. In later visits to East Asia during the 1990s, I could see the economic domino effect at work among what were called the Asian Tigers and how it was spreading to yet more Asian countries. During the 1960s Egypt's GDP was higher than South Korea's, but today South Korea is among the top ten economies in the world while Egypt suffers hugely. We can see how China decided to become an economic power rather than risk collapse like the Soviet Union. It has done this under Communist Party rule and I believe that China will face challenges from within to one-party rule. India's economy is vibrant and some African countries are now coming into their own. Parts of the Arab world, however, are going backwards, riven by sectarian conflicts fuelled by internal and external vested interests.

The Arab world will need a strong leadership that will set an inspirational course, and like great leaders who have created nations from nothing this will require huge risks and sacrifice. But it will be worth it and future generations will be thankful for those responsible.

As Arab nations move forwards, freedom, accountability and economic prosperity will not be easy to achieve after years of bad governance. Transformation will not happen without a deter-mined leadership that means well for its people and their future. Arab men and women need to believe that they are born free and will remain free to think, live, choose the life they like and say what they like – and will be rewarded for hard work within an effective institutional system that meets their expectations and protects their rights. If this does not happen, I do not see a stable future ahead.

NOTES

1 1970–2011: four decades of transformation in the Gulf

1 'Saudi Arabia: Education', Library of Congress, Federal Research Division, Country Studies.
2 'Economic development in the UAE', Mohamed Shihab.
3 'Saudi Arabia: Economy', op. cit.
4 'Gulf world's fifth largest economy by 2020', *Arabian Business*, 5 July 2008.
5 'GCC's non-oil sector expected to grow at 6.4%', *Emirates Business 24/7*, 23 December 2008.
6 Ibid.
7 'Red tape hinders investments in GCC,' *Emirates Business 24–7*, 12 March 2008.
8 www.doingbusiness.org, World Bank website
9 'Saudi border checks push up prices in Qatar', www.MENAFN.com, 29 September 2009.
10 'Sovereign-wealth funds', *The Economist*, 17 January 2008.
11 'Poverty a major problem for Arab world', *Gulf News*, 13 January 2011.
12 'Arab world experiences rapid population explosion', *World Focus*, 23 March 2011.
13 Ibid.

2 *The Arab spring*

1   'How wired are the Middle East and North Africa?', CNN.
2   Ibid.
3   'Assad cousin accused of favouring family', *Financial Times*, 21
    April 2011.
4   International Organization for Migration, Migration and
    Development in Egypt.
5   The World Bank.
6   '30% decline in Arab workers number in the Gulf', *Egypt News*,
    29 March 2009.
7   CIA World Factbook.
8   'Egypt's military discourages economic change', *New York Times*,
    17 February 2011.

3 *Economic diversification in the GCC: the rentier state*

1   H. Beblawi, 'The Rentier State in the Arab World', in H.
    Beblawi and G. Luciani (eds), *The Rentier State*, Croom Helm,
    1987, Chapter 2.
2   In economics, the term 'rent' is used to refer not just to the
    income from ownership of land or property – as is the case in
    popular usage – but also any incomes derived as a result of prices
    being in excess of production costs. Revenues from hydrocarbon
    extraction are therefore, in economic terms, regarded as rent.
3   H. Beblawi, op. cit.
4   U. Fasano and Q. Wang, 'Fiscal Expenditure Policy and Non-Oil
    Economic Growth: Evidence from the GCC Countries', IMF
    Working Paper, December 2001.
5   P. Stevens, 'Resource Impact: Curse or Blessing? A Literature
    Survey', *Journal of Energy Literature*, vol. 9, no. 1, 2003, pp. 1–42.
6   T. Stauffer, 'Income Measurement in Arab States', in H. Beblawi
    and G. Luciani (eds), op. cit., Chapter 1.

7   O. Noreng, 'The Predicament of the Gulf Rentier State', in
    D. Heradstveit and H. Hveem (eds), *Oil In the Gulf*, Ashgate
    Publishing, 2004, Chapter 1.

8   John W. Fox, Nada Mourtada Sabbah and Mohammed
    Al Mutawa, 'Traditionalism globalized or globalization
    traditionalized?', in John W. Fox, Nada Mourtada Sabbah
    and Mohammed Al Mutawa (eds), *Globalization and the Gulf*,
    Routledge, 2006, Chapter 1.

9   See, for example, www.guardian.co.uk/world/2008/oct/08/
    middleeast.construction

10 U. Fasano and Z. Iqbal, *GCC Countries: From Oil Dependence to
    Diversification*, IMF, 2003.

11 See, for example, W.A. Lewis, 'Economic Development with
    Unlimited Supplies of Labour', *The Manchester School 232*, 1954,
    pp. 139–91, for the classic model of this type.

12 Christopher Clague, Philip Keefer, Stephen Knack and Mancur
    Olsen, 'Democracy, Autocracy, and the Institutions Supportive
    of Economic Growth', in C. Clague (ed), *Institutions and Economic
    Development: Growth and Governance in Less-Developed and Post-
    Socialist Countries*, Johns Hopkins University Press, 1997, pp.
    91–120.

13 M. Khan, 'What Is a "Good Investment Climate"?', in Gudrun
    Kochendorfer-Lucius and Boris Pleskovic (eds), *Investment
    Climate, Growth, and Poverty*, World Bank Publications, 2005.

14 M. Noland and H. Pack, *The Arab Economies in a Changing World*,
    Peterson Institute for International Economics, 2007, p. 31.

4 *Economic reform*

1   IMF, *Direction of Trade Statistics Database*, Washington, DC, 2011.

2   OECD, *What is the Economic Outlook for OECD Countries? An
    Interim Assessment of the OECD Economic Outlook*, Paris, September
    2011.

3   OPEC, *Annual Statistical Bulletin*, Vienna, 2010/11.

4   World Economic Forum, *The Global Competitiveness Report*
     2011–2012, 2011.
5   H. Mahdavi, 'The Patterns and Problems of Economic
     Development in Rentier States', in M. Cook (ed), *Studies in
     Economic History of the Middle East*, Oxford University Press, 1970.
6   G. Luciani, 'Allocation vs. Production States: A Theoretical
     Framework', in G. Luciani (ed), *The Arab State*, University of
     California Press, 1990.
7   G. Luciani, 'Resources, Revenues, and Authoritarianism in the
     Arab World: Beyond the Rentier State', in R. Brynen, B. Korany
     and P. Noble (eds), *Political Liberalization and Democratization in the
     Arab World: Theoretical Perspectives*, Lynne Rienner, 1995.
8   K.A. Chaudhry, 'The Price of Wealth: Economies and
     Institutions in the Middle East', Cornell University Press, 1997.
9   B. Smith, 'Oil Wealth and Regime Survival in the Developing
     World, 1960–1999', *American Journal of Political Science*, vol. 48, no.
     2, April 2004.
10   The Gulf, Economics of Knowledge, 2011.
11   S. Shochat, *The Gulf Cooperation Council Economies: Diversification
     and Reform: An Introduction*, London School of Economics, 2008.
12   IMF, *Economic Transformation in MENA1. Delivering on the Promise of
     Shared Prosperity*, Washington, DC, 2011.
13   The World Bank, *Global Entrepreneurship Monitor: MENA Regional
     Report*, Cairo, 2010.
14   The World Bank, *From Privilege to Competition: Unlocking Private-
     led Growth in the Middle East and North Africa*, 2009.
15   IMF, *Economic Transformation in MENA*, op. cit.
16   J. Calderwood, 'Western universities opening in GCC "at risk of
     failing"', *The National*, 4 April 2011.
17   The World Bank, *Group Entrepreneurship Snapshots. Finance and
     Private Sector Research*, Washington, DC, 2010.
18   IMF, *Regional Economic Outlook, Middle East and Central Asia*,
     April 2011.
19   International Labour Office, 'Growth, Employment and Decent
     Work in the Arab Region: Key Policy Issues', *Arab Employment
     Forum*, Beirut, October 2009.

20 IMF, *Middle East and North Africa Region: Job Creation in an Era of High Growth*, 2007.

21 International Organisation for Migration, *Egypt after January 25: Survey of Youth Migration Intentions*, Cairo, 2011.

22 International Intellectual Property Alliance, *Report on Copyright Protection and Enforcement* (Special 301 Report), 2011.

23 S. Hertog, *Two-level negotiations in a fragmented system: Saudi Arabia's WTO accession*, 8 November 2008. Retrieved 21 October 2011 from London School of Economics and Political Science: http://eprints.lse.ac.uk/29862/1/Saudi_Arabia_and_the_WTO_(LSERO).pdf

24 'Saudi Arabia to Take Part in First Arab Consumer and Brand Protection Forum', *Khaleej Times*, 19 October 2007.

25 J. Heintz, and G. Chang, *Statistics on Employment in the Informal Sector and Informal Employment: A Summary of Updated Estimates from the ILO Bureau of Statistics Database*, ILO Employment Sector, 2009.

5 Political reform

1 F.G. Gause, 'Why Middle East Studies Missed the Arab Spring', *Foreign Affairs*, July 2011.

2 Jerome Taylor, 'How Britain taught Arab police forces all they know', *The Independent*, 19 February 2011.

3 M. Lynch, 'Globalization and Arab Security', in J. Kirshner (ed), *Globalization and National Security*, Routledge, 2006, pp. 171–200.

4 Z. Autio and E. Acs, *The Global Entrepreneurship and Development Index: A Brief Explanation*, Imperial College and George Mason University, 2010.

5 W. Ghonim: www.facebook.com/ElShaheeed

6 B. Rubin, 'Pan-Arab Nationalism: The Ideological Dream as a Compelling Force', *Journal of Contemporary History*, vol. 26, no. 3/4, 1991.

7 Arab Financial Forum, *Arab Financial Forum Newsletter*, September 2011.

8   'Revolution spinning in the wind', *The Economist*, July 2011.

9   Ibid.

10 G. Abdul-Ahad, 'Inside Syria: lightly armed townsfolk take on tanks as army closes in', *The Guardian*, 9 December 2011.

11 O. Roy, *Holy Ignorance: When Religion and Culture Part Ways*, Columbia University Press, 2009.

12 A. Christie-Mille, 'Erdogan pitches Turkey's democratic model on "Arab Spring" tour', *The Christian Science Monitor*, 16 September 2011.

13 G. Perrier, 'Turkish authorities launch raids to censor book before publication', *The Guardian*, 5 April 2011.

14 M. Guida, 'The New Islamist Understanding of Democracy in Turkey', *Turkish Studies*, vol. 12, no. 3, 2011.

BIBLIOGRAPHY

Hamoush Ahmad, 'A Week of Disturbances Besieges al-Fassi Government,' IslamOnline.net, January 2011.

'Salary Hike Comes After a Day of Protest: Jordan Hikes Govt Salaries in Face of Discontent', Al Arabiya News Channel, 21 January 2011.

'Algeria Democracy Rally Broken Up: Several Injured as Police Disperse 300 People Who Defied a Ban and Attempted to Demonstrate in Capital', Al Jazeera, 22 January 2011.

Abdullah Baaboud, 'Dynamics and Determinants of the GCC States' Foreign Policy, with Special Reference to the EU', in Gerd Nunneman (ed), *Analyzing Middle Eastern Foreign Policy*, Routledge, 2007, pp. 145–73.

Joel Beinin, 'Underbelly of Egypt New Neoliberal Agenda', *Middle East Report*, 5 April 2008.

Hazem Beblawi, 'The Rentier State in the Arab World', in Giacomo Luciani (ed), *The Arab State*, Routledge, 1990, pp. 85–98.

N. Chamlou, *The Environment for Women's Entrepreneurship in the Middle East and North Africa*, The World Bank, 2008.

Christopher M. Davidson, 'Persian Gulf – Pacific Asia Linkages in the 21st Century: A Marriage of Convenience?', Kuwait

Programme on Development, Governance, and Globalisation, London School of Economics, 2010.

Hossam el-Hamalawy, 'Strikes in Egypt Spread From Center of Gravity', *Middle East Report*, 9 May 2011.

David Held, 'Democracy: the Nation State and the Global System', in Malcolm Waters (ed), *Modernity: Critical Concepts*, vol. 4, 'After Modernity', Routledge, 2001, pp. 411–45.

Noha el-Hennawy, 'Egypt's Opposition Seeks to Translate Social Discontent Before Elections', *Al-Masry Al-Youm*, 5 October 2010.

Martin Hvidt, 'The Dubai Model: An Outline of Key Development-Process Elements in Dubai', *International Journal of Middle East Studies*, vol. 41, no. 3, 2009, pp. 397–418.

IMF, *Direction of Trade Statistics Database*, 2011.

IMF, *World Economic Outlook Database*, September 2011.

'Multilateralism and Global Governance: Accountability and Effectiveness' in David Held and David Mepham (eds), *Progressive Foreign Policy: New Directions for the UK*, Polity Press, 2007, pp. 191–212.

Terry Karl, *The Paradox of Plenty: Oil Booms and Petrostates*, University of California Press, 1997.

Malcolm Kerr and Yasin al-Sayyid, *Rich and Poor States in the Middle East: Egypt and the New Arab Order*, Westview Press, 1982.

L. Klapper, *Entrepreneurship and the Financial Crisis: An Overview of the 2010 Entrepreneurship Snapshots (WBGES)*, World Bank Development Research Group, 2010.

Joseph Kostiner, *Middle East Monarchies: The Challenge of Modernity*, Lynne Rienner, 2000.

R. Lee and A. Mason, 'What Is the Demographic Dividend?', *Finance and Development*, vol. 43, no. 3, IMF, 2006.

Marc Lynch, 'Globalisation and Arab Security' in Jonathan Kirshner (ed), *Globalisation and National Security*, Routledge, 2006, pp. 171–200.

Kevin Morrison, 'Oil, Non-Tax Revenue, and Regime Stability: The Political Resource Curse Re-examined', in Harvard University Comparative Political Economy Workshop, 2005.

Khaldoun Hasan al-Naqeeb, *Society and State in the Gulf and Arab Peninsula: A Different Perspective*, translated by L.M. Kenny, Routledge, 1990.

Tim Niblock and Monica Malik, *The Political Economy of Saudi Arabia*, Routledge, 2007.

OECD, *MENA Initiative on Governance and Investment for Development*, 2011.

Samir Ranjan Pradhan, 'GCC-Asia Relations: Intensifying Cooperation Beyond Mutual Interdependence', in Abdulaziz Sager (ed), *Gulf Yearbook 2008–2009*, Gulf Research Centre, 2009, pp. 157–73.

Vincent Romani, 'The Politics of Higher Education in the Middle East: Problems and Prospects', *Middle East Brief 36*, Crown Center for Middle East Studies, Brandeis University, 2009.

Abdulaziz Sager, 'The G20 Meeting and Gulf Interests', Gulf Research Centre, www.grc.ae, accessed 23 August 2011.

Mohamed El-Sayed Said, 'Global Civil Society: An Arab Perspective' in Helmut Anheier, Marlies Glasius and Mary Kaldor (eds), *Global Civil Society Yearbook 2004/5*, Sage, 2004, pp. 60–73.

Ahmed Abdelkareem Saif, 'Deconstructing Before Building: Perspectives on Democracy in Qatar', in Steven Wright and Anoushiravan Ehteshami (eds), *Reform in the Middle East Oil Monarchies*, Ithaca Press, 2008.

Rolf Schwarz, 'State Formation Processes in Rentier States: The Middle Eastern Case', in Fifth Pan-European Conference on International Relations – 'International Relations Meet Area Studies', ECPR Standing Group on International Relations, Section 34, 9–11 September 2004.

Jillian Schwedler, 'More Than a Mob: the Dynamics of Political Demonstrations in Jordan', *Middle East Report*, no. 226, April 2011.

Mark Smith, 'Russia and the Persian Gulf: The Deepening of Moscow's Middle East Policy', Middle East Series Paper, Conflict Studies Research Centre, Defence Academy of the United Kingdom, 2007.

Bibliography

'Workers' Leadership Forms Preparatory Committee for Workers', *The Socialist*, Center for Socialist Studies, 1 July 2009.

'The Struggle for Workers' Rights in Egypt', Solidarity Center Report, www.solidaritycenter.org/files/pubs_egypt_wr.pdf, p. 15.

Joshua Teitelbaum, 'Understanding Political Liberalisation in the Gulf: An Introduction', in Joshua Teitelbaum (ed), *Political Liberalisation in the Persian Gulf*, Columbia University Press, 2008.

Mary Ann Tetreault, 'Kuwait Annus Mirabilis', *Middle East Report*, 17 September 2006.

Transparency International, *Corruption Perceptions Index 2010*.

UN Development Programme, Regional Bureau for Arab States, *The Arab Human Development Report 2005: Towards the Rise of Women in the Arab World*, United Nations, 2005.

UN Development Programme, Regional Bureau for Arab States, *Arab Human Development Report 2009: Challenges to Human Security in Arab Countries*, United Nations Publications, 2009.

Rodney Wilson, 'Economic Governance and Reform in Saudi Arabia', in Anoushiravan Ehteshami and Steven M. Wright (eds), *Reform in the Middle East Oil Monarchies*, Ithaca Press, 2008, pp. 132–52.

World Bank, *MENA: Creation of a Regional Infrastructure Regulatory Forum*, 2010.

World Bank, World Development Indicators and Global Development Finance Database, 2011.

World Bank, Towards a New Partnership for Inclusive Growth in the MENA Region, 2011.

Douglas Yates, *The Rentier State in Africa: Oil Rent Dependency and Neo-colonialism in the Republic of Gabon*, Africa World Press, 1996.

INDEX

banking
and the 2008 financial crisis 18
conservativism 18, 26
Sharia-compliant 18
and SMEs 100–101
in Tunisia 66–7
Ben Ali, Zine el-Abidine 13, 71, 75, 99
Benghazi, Libya 22, 86
Bern Convention (1971) 65
borders
earlier ease of crossing xxii
movement of goods 5
open 5
Bouazizi, Muhammad 69–70
brain drain 10, 60
British army 71
British rule 1, 93
budget expenditure 100
Bulac, Ali 89
bureaucracy 5, 17, 25, 28, 80
Burj Khalifa tower, Dubai 3
Business Software Alliance 62

Cairo 81, 82
Camp David agreement (1978) 99
capital formation 29, 43
capital markets 26, 47
capitalism 32
crony 40
Cedar Revolution (2005) 79
China 5, 42, 108–9
Chinese Communist Party 108
citizenship 50, 108
civil service 44

civil society xiii, 22, 66, 68, 97, 104
Cold War 10
colonial rule 9
communism, and Islamism 10
comparative advantage 52
competition 5, 10, 39
competitive advantage 29, 52
competitiveness 18, 30, 45, 60, 61, 99
construction 36, 37
consumerism xxiii, 32, 33
corruption 10, 13, 16–17, 20, 25, 69, 72, 74, 76, 78, 79, 82, 95, 96, 97, 99, 105
Council of Ministers (Saudi Arabia) 64
credit 37, 39
crony capitalism 40
cronyism 46

Damascus, Syria 85
Davutoglu, Ahmet 86
decision-making
informal 9
lack of transparency 5
political and security factors 5
democracy 78, 83, 94, 97
and Arab revolutionaries 80
concept of 70
in Egypt 82
and fiscal association 49
Fukuyama on 96
lack of 10
in Lebanon and Iraq 85
in Libya 21

Index

becomes more powerful and
confident 4
and bureaucracy 28
dysfunctional 17
impediments to growth 5
incentives to kick-starting 74
interlinked with education and
institutional reform 53
job creation in 102
mirroring the public sector 18
and oligarchy 18
pay 41
rebalancing 53
privatisation 55, 59, 60, 74, 75, 76,
99–100
productivity 6, 31, 67, 102
property
freehold 11
private 26
real estate prices 4, 36
rights xiii, 61–5, 97, 102
protectionism 25
public sector
absorption of job seekers 17,
35
and bureaucracy 28
employment dominated by
102
job creation in 42
patronage 17
pay 41, 42
rebalancing 53
undemanding jobs in xxi, 104

Qaddafi, Muammar 13, 22
Qaddafi family 74

Qatar
agriculture xxii
boycott of Qtel 84
communications xvii, xxi–xxii
development programme xxii
diet in early 20th century xvii
education xx, xxi, xxii–xxiii,
54, 56, 59
financial centre 37
foreign workers in xxii
friction with Saudi Arabia 5
independence (1971) 1
and the knowledge sector 52
large LNG producer xi
liberalisation projects 51
limited police force and lack of
crime xix
a major oil exporter 73–4
Ministry of Economy and
Trade xi, xii
Ministry of Education
(Department of Knowledge)
xvi
natural gas production 36
patents 63
private-sector activity 48
reaction to events of Arab
spring 102
rentier state 49–50
research and development 101
start of oil revenues (1960s) xv
state building 1
television in xvii–xviii
transporting water xix–xx
understood the forces behind
the Arab spring 107–8

··· 131 ···

revolution of 2011 15, 16, 21,
   79
sectarian and tribal divisions 14
security services 81
Shia in 98
Sunnis' attitude to Shias 22
unemployment 46
violent tactics 105
Syrian army 73

Taiwan 53
tariffs 25
taxation 30–31, 40, 44
television channels 16
Thailand 5
tourism 3, 5, 36, 38
Trabelsi, Leila 17
Trabelsi family 18
trade unions 22
Trade-Related Aspects of
   Intellectual Property Rights
   (TRIPs) 64, 65
transit fees 48
transparency 5, 8–9, 25, 26, 98,
   104, 108
transport
   air xxii
   animal xix
   car xix, xxi
   sea xxii
tribalism 14, 22–3, 103
Tunis 81
Tunisia 85
   banking 66–7
   Ben Ali overthrown 13
   challenges to the old guards 81

corruption 99
economic reforms backfire on
   government 75
governance 17
inherited economic woes 76
internet access 16
job creation 106
lack of economic or political
   improvements 10
leaderless popular mobilisation
   in 77
the military 72
new government 94
oil output 45
religious parties 20, 24
remittances 18
revolution (2011) 13, 16, 18, 21,
   22, 55, 66, 69, 75, 78, 79, 80,
   84, 89–90
unemployment 46
US embassy cables 16–17
Tunisian army 72
Turkey 80
   AK Party 75, 86–7, 89
   building of more open and
      democratic system 70
   deep-rooted secular order 87–8
   and democracy 86, 96
   economic reforms 75
   intervention in Arab politics 14
   Islamism 86–9
   killing of nine Turks by Israeli
      commandos 88
   military role in 24, 25
   relationship with Iran 87
   role in the region 21